Yes I Can

Learn to use the Power of Self-efficacy

By Dr. Laura Ritchie

Published in the United Kingdom by:

Effic Research Limited
7 Torriano Mews
London
NW5 2RZ

ISBN: 978-1-9997943-4-7

This is for you.

"She stares into the sun"
Oil on canvas by Catherine Ritchie, 2020

Contents

Foreword

Sammy Davis wrote a book called "Yes I Can." I sent him a wire, said "No you can't." Frank Sinatra, "Tea Break," *Sinatra at the Sands* (1966)

Frank was joking. But sometimes people do tell us, "no you can't." Chapter 6 of this new book by Laura Ritchie tackles this challenge head-on. She provides readers with insight into others' critical comments and a checklist of strategies for dealing with them.

But this is not the main point of her book. Professor Ritchie has not written a *"Handbook of What to do When Other People Say 'No, You Can't.'"*

Sometimes we *tell ourselves* "no, *I* can't." We pay attention to our self, our challenges, and our possibilities and become *self*-doubters. In the lingo of psychological science, we develop low "self-efficacy" beliefs.

For those of you skeptical of lingo, I'll provide a quick overview. "Perceived Self-Efficacy" is not a pop psychology term. It is a product of psychological science – that place where men and women are called "males" and "females"; the situations they encounter are called "experimental conditions"; and their actions and experiences are "dependent variables." It might seem to take all the fun out of psychology, but the dry, cold, objective procedures of psychological science are the same type of dry, cold procedures that give you, for example, faith in a new COVID-19 vaccine. In other words, they have got a lot going for them. The scientific effort lurking in the background of Dr. Ritchie's new book is particularly thorough. "Self-efficacy" was introduced by the renowned Stanford University psychologist Albert Bandura in a publication that – if I've got my numbers right – is the singularly most highly cited paper in the 127-year history of psychology's premier scientific journal. Self-efficacy theory, in turn, is a major component of Bandura's overall Social Cognitive Theory – a theoretical framework so widely influential that (if I've got these numbers right, too) Bandura is now the contemporary world's most highly cited scholar in any field.

Somehow, Dr. Ritchie succeeds in conveying the essence of the self-efficacy literature without forcing the reader to slog through scientific details. The latter sections of Chapter 5, "Motivation," are a particularly cogent presentation of a key feature of social cognitive theory: the back-and-forth interactions (the "loop," as Dr. Ritchie put it) among people's experiences of success and failure, beliefs in their efficacy for future success, and deeper feelings about themselves as learners with potential. We see here – and in many other chapters of this book – the power of self-efficacy.

Yet, I'm not sure that's the main point of the book, either. True, discussions of how self-doubt inhibits success and self-efficacy powers appears on many pages. And it does say "power of self-efficacy" right there in the subtitle on the cover. But maybe you can't tell the book by its cover. Consider a passage in Chapter 2, "Life's Maze." While discussing social cognitive theory's analysis of "yes, you can," Ritchie writes about a *different* psychological process that "is less explicitly a part of the psychological theory of how people function socially as thinkers" (i.e., social cognitive theory). This something different is "*meta*cognition . . . which happens *before and after* the decision that yes, you can do something" (emphases added).

Metacognition is awareness. It is an active noticing of your own thoughts. But, as we learn from *Yes I Can*, it's more than that. Your thoughts are generally directed out to the world: the world in front of you now, the one you experienced yesterday, and the possible worlds of the future. Metacognition thus is awareness of your awareness of, in essence, everything. Insufficient metacognition – a lack of awareness of your processes of thinking – is significant. It can constitute a failure to recognize possibilities that might be right in front of you. "Metacognitive awareness" thus is not just eight syllables of psychobabble. It is, Dr. Ritchie instructs, a key ingredient in the recipe for success. Not only reaching one's dreams but also formulating them in the first place requires "an active awareness of our selves and our surroundings." Experiences can "[wake] the need to realize, pay attention, and look for things." You can learn "awareness and openness . . . from young children." "The key to findings your 'yes' is in being aware." "Becoming aware . . . is about incorporating the pause that inhibits habit." "Awareness and thinking equip us to make choices." "Noticing and realizing is the first step." "Begin to notice." "See differently."

In saying all this, Professor Ritchie incorporates and *transcends* the social cognitive theory that is her home base. Her psychological claims echo not so much Bandura as the classic texts of Buddhists, for whom awareness and active attention – "right mindfulness" – is a spoke on the dharmachakra. They align with contemporary psychology's "mindfulness" movement, where awareness of oneself and one's surroundings is key to well-being. As writing, her prose echoes authors of the Beat Generation, whose fundament goal was to expand conscious awareness of the world's wonders. They echo also the writing of David Foster

Wallace, who – in the most brilliant of commencement addresses – instructed graduates that "The really important kind of freedom involves attention and awareness and discipline, and being able truly to care about other people and to sacrifice for them over and over in myriad petty, unsexy ways every day. That is real freedom. That is being educated, and understanding how to think. The alternative is unconsciousness, the default setting, the rat race." Like Wallace, Ritchie wants us to switch out of autopilot. To think about our thoughts. To think about the thoughts we haven't thought yet. She teaches by instruction and by example – example after example in which our Author displays keen awareness of wonders that pass most people by.

In her writing, Dr. Ritchie aims for simplicity. (It is "attractive and approachable.") She achieves it. Yet her book is perhaps *deceptively* simple. If you just breeze through it – a pleasant story about children here, something about growing carrots there, some self-efficacy theory, a bit about British Bumble Bees – you might become confident that you've learned the book's lessons while its subtleties and complexities pass you by. Do you really want to learn the lessons of *Yes I Can*? Learning requires work. You have to pay attention, connect dots, ask why things are happening, ask yourself how you feel about what's happening, realize you might be missing something, and try to figure out what that something is. And *that's* the main point of the book, at least as I read it. Learning to use the power of self-efficacy requires more than just saying "Yes I Can." Learning requires work. Effort. Awareness. Concentrated attention.

Hmm, maybe you *can* tell the book by its cover. There's our Author. She's not leaping about shouting "Yes I Can." She's the picture of concentrated attention.

Daniel Cervone
Professor of Psychology, University of Illinois at Chicago

Introduction

As time passes, plants grow. They grow *up*. It doesn't matter whether they are in the forest or the city, what the conditions are, whether the day is cloudy or clear, whether someone might step on them or eat them; no matter how inhospitable the conditions the plants grow up. They reach for the stars. Quite literally they reach for our star, the sun. The plant somehow finds no boundary in the fact that it may not rain, it may be scorched, it still reaches and continues to grow with every fibre it has.

I want to be like that. Do you want to be like that? Of course we need to be aware of the body's needs for food, water, and sleep, but beyond that, can it be done? Can I grow like the simple blades of grass, the dandelions that without fail, pop up and bloom? Actually, yes I can. It is such an easy little phrase to say, but there is so much in it. To externally say, to name, to begin to manifest this takes considerable belief, strength, and commitment to your goal. It means the acknowledgement of possibility and the willingness to reach, to traverse and navigate the unknown.

In psychology, self-efficacy is the belief in our capabilities to do a specific task. It is a belief in both now and future. It is a belief in you. Self-efficacy is about capacity to realise opportunity, that is to say – a belief about making the possible reality. It takes you from where you are now, whatever skill, level, place on the road where you find yourself, and it asks you to have vision. Can I? Yes, I can.

Look around you:

The plants that grow *reach*. They do this regardless, despite, and always – without vision or judgement. By nature they reach unceasingly, which is both wonderful and mysterious. This is our inspiration. It is a challenge though, because as people, we have doubt. Does the dandelion think itself less valuable than the rose, and decide to wither because it is a weed? No. It has the resilience of a dozen roses. When we find our yes and learn to reach, we too can grow with resilience and confidence. We can break free from the many influences and forces that might seem beyond our control, from cultural expectations, to societal values, people who are big bosses, and even random strangers. We can see beyond the habit that allows us to be derailed by the power of a cold stare or a single word. The toxicity of 'no', 'can't', and 'don't' will become dim in your memory and leave your vocabulary to be replaced by a vision of possibility and growth.

Yes I Can is about understanding our perspective, our self-beliefs, our situation, how and what we *can* do, and looking at the art of making this a fundamental part of who you are, your way of life. This is more than a mindset. It is about understanding the processes underlying your decision making about your capabilities and self-beliefs, and how to allow and enable yourself to move from wherever you are through the vision of possibility to achieving your goals. Strategic thinking, instead of grit or willpower, will serve you as you align yourself to adopt the yes into your daily life.

We are far more than either the dandelion or the rose. Neither of these is capable of vision, but we can perceive our surroundings and can dream our future. Somehow even without hope, without goals, these flowers still grow. How much more can you grow? We have a powerful capacity to understand, interact, and indeed dream, and this vision can be focused through many lenses. It is true that for each of us there are barriers to belief and achievement, however, many of the biggest walls are not as immovable as they seem. Many seemingly real roadblocks in fact stem from our own minds, from perceptions that we have cultivated and allowed to build over time.

It's time to tidy up the garden, relearn how to grow, and embrace the *Yes I Can*.

Author's note: Why me?

Although my PhD was in psychology of music studying people's self-efficacy and designing ways to understand specific beliefs about learning and performing in music, and I am now a chartered psychologist, I have never been *formally* trained in psychology. By nature I am a thinker and life has pointed me in the direction of learning to think and understand others in a way that is rather outside most people's experience and expectations. As a child I asked two questions of all adults. (I was an only child and so was trailed around wherever my parents went, and I mostly spoke with adults.) I always asked these two questions: 'What are you thinking? and Tell me a story?' I think the second question diffused the first, but because I was aged 4-6 most people would answer me, and surprisingly they spoke with elements of honestly, probably because I was a child. I soaked in whatever I could. I woke early and would sit at the window listening and watching the birds and squirrels in the early morning light, dancing in the backyard. I learned to see and hear.

What does this have to do with self-efficacy? With this book? I learned it, I lived it, and because of the combination of my keen observation skills and the training in critical thinking I received early on in school, I was in a unique position to notice it all happening as it unfolded. I kept finding myself in situations where everything was new, not just tasks, but literally everything. After my undergrad degree, I moved to the UK. I followed love, and also the cello. I remember packing my bags, the limit of what you could carry on the airplane, and that was it really. I left family, friends, country, and despite speaking what I thought was English, I found myself a foreigner in a new land. Every task was a test. *Every* thing was new. I had to learn not just to hear, but to listen, and to understand the mechanisms at work in communication, intention, motives – all sorts of interplay that mixed into the cocktail of everyday interaction.

As I didn't exactly fit culturally, I did look with different eyes, and was allowed to have a slightly altered perspective – I was a quirky anomaly. What that did mean, was I chose what I did. There was a conscious planning, choosing, and strategy for achieving what I wanted to do. The path in front of me was not obvious, there was no predestination or expectation of what I would become or where I would go, and I approached life with the freedom and expectation that I would do it. I wasn't always sure what 'it' was, but I was jolly well going to do it. What have I done? I have now written four degrees, a Foundation Degree in Instrumental and Vocal Teaching, a BA in Instrumental and Vocal Teaching, an MA in Performance, and a Postgraduate

Certificate in Teaching Instruments and Voice. I have been recognized for innovation in teaching with a UK National Teaching Fellowship. I wrote my PhD thesis Musical Self-efficacy for Learning and Performing as a part time student, while lecturing full time and having my third child. I have spoken on self-efficacy, the psychology of learning and teaching, and innovation in North America, South America, and across Europe. I play my cello and have composed and recorded the original soundtrack to a feature length documentary film, performed with a band at Glastonbury and on the Jools Holland show, give regular recitals, and have done wacky things like take dozens of students to do a flashmob at a traditional video arcade in rural Virginia. Just because I can. I also step outside traditional expectations for a Professor of Learning and Teaching and take students to LA where last year we went axe throwing as well as performed a jazz set in a cozy club (I was singing wearing platform heels and a little black dress – who would have thought it of this 40+ mum of three professor!?).

In this book I use examples of moments when I learned about the can, and also the times where I was told I can't, and sometimes I believed them. My hope is that through telling some of these stories and explaining what's behind them, you will be able to find your *'can'* too, and unlike me, it won't take you 20 years after some of the experiences to figure it out. The stories presented are like a framework for you. We are all people doing our lives for the first time, and to be honest I do not know what's around the corner. The point is, as an expert learner and a very good communicator, I know *I can* and I believe you can too.

CHAPTER ONE
Awareness of Yes and the Self

A story…

Every week I meet with a group of people who come together to form an orchestra. I know very little about the people. I have no idea where they come from, what their jobs are, if they have jobs, what they believe, like or dislike, what they eat for dinner, what they do or have done in their lives, and yet we do amazing things together.

We framed our first concert as an informal playing of our pieces: anyone can come, it's free, share bring food and drink, and we make music. We played in the University Chapel which is very beautiful, but it is a big, big space with two giant stained glass walls that was built before people thought of insulation or heat retention, and let's just say that can be a challenge. Winter in England can mean a cold and wet that gets into your bones. Once we got there, there was no problem. The place was packed! With 100+ bodies in the audience – and 46 more people listed as performers on the programme, the heating was no problem.

What's so special about this group?

We do it. We make music and it actually sounds good and it's not conventional and it's not your usual group makeup, and sod that, we do it anyway and I have not remembered a more purely joyful collaborative concert experience in a very long time.

It's not about right notes or perfection. It's about growth -- being a part of, and letting music be the medium that carried us and the audience. This music had meaning because everyone in the space cared about each other and collectively worked to make it come together. It wasn't primarily about the sounds, but about the accomplishments, the audacity of someone to believe that after however many years of not playing they could do it again, that even though they never did a grade whatever or maybe never played with others that they could. You can. You bloody well can, and I'm not going to tell you otherwise. I am going to do everything I can to find a way to help you to do it.

Childhood awareness

When children are young they are surrounded with all things new, and it seems so natural to question and experience what the world has to offer in every way possible. Children watch, listen, do - experiment, explore, express, feel and they do this both independently and by reaching out to others. From the moment a child is born and takes that first, powerful and effortful breath, they are constantly moving and reaching for whatever lies beyond, even before it is possible to know what could be there or formulate and articulate any specific desires or goals. Negotiating the world gives children experience with their own physicality, the physical makeup of this world, temporality and existing within the bounds of time, and crucially, interactions with others.

Up to about the age of three years old, children do not have an understanding of the divide between thinking and saying, or between what *they* know and what someone else can perceive. A toddler cannot comprehend the idea of private thoughts, and the sense of awareness that separates and enables a critical comparison between their thoughts (what they personally know) and how that is separate from outwardly communicated ideas. For them that cognitive awareness has not yet developed and as a result nothing is hidden. I first saw this concept demonstrated on a BBC documentary with the popular medical doctor and scientist Robert Winston some fifteen years ago. Parents were filmed asking children to play the common game of hiding something in one of their hands and having the adult guess which hand had contained the item. Generally with this game the person doing the hiding starts with their hands behind their back, secretly conceals the object in one hand, and presents two closed fists to the onlooker, leaving them unaware of the object's location, and making it genuinely a guessing game. When the young child is asked to do this, because they do not understand the boundary between private and public, everything is on show, but they do not realize they have given away the game. They just cannot do it and *think* they are playing the game successfully. They young child has no clue their opponent is already aware of the object's location. The idea of 'hiding' is just foreign to them.

When I first saw this experiment I was incensed and couldn't believe this could be true, so I thought I would test this game with my own children. At the time my children were just over 4 and 2 ½, and I thought they were both quite clever. I anticipated no problems at all with this little game. The eldest could indeed play the game fine, but when I asked my younger child to play the same game, giving the same instructions, sure enough they couldn't do it! I was presented with a lovely sweet open hand, showing me a shiny penny and asking, 'Which one?' Even after re-explaining they should put their hands behind their back first to stop me seeing where the penny is, the same outcome resulted – with the slight change that this time the penny and both hands started behind their back and then were presented, in full sight, for me to guess where it was. This unfiltered way of thinking would not be an ideal quality to retain, and children quickly grow mentally and physically, beginning to develop more and more of that sense of self. However, while young, these children do literally learn out loud, and watching their unashamed learning gives us a window into their thought processes. There is a great deal we can learn and re-learn from observing how children experience the world.

The importance of others and the role they play in learning and development cannot be underestimated or ignored. The people closest to us, family and others we come into contact with in our daily lives, have both direct and indirect influence on the way we make sense of ourselves and our surroundings.

Children have no problem co-existing, connecting, and living in the presence of one another. Wherever they are, whoever they are with, whatever things they have or do not have, children notice and explore. Children learn out loud, in the open. Partly this is by design as their cognitive awareness, physical development, and assimilation of the two in their general functioning are all far from complete. Inside their brains schema and new neural pathways are formed constantly, and physically bones and muscles grow, resulting in a continuously changing situation that almost requires an active and genuine exploration of their 'selves' in this world.

It is true that children do not start out with a comprehension or regard for societal rules or limits within nearly every aspect of life, and especially public life, but somehow their naïveté in combination with a sincere and bold drive to learn encourages a softening of the usual rules. It is neither scandalous when babies put toys in their mouths nor are toddlers looked upon as clumsy fools when they fall down. Instead a public reaction is more likely for some stranger to smile and perhaps even reach out to offer a big hand to help that little person get back on their feet. When interacting with the very young, there is sometimes a spark-like connection that harks back to that innocent and authentic way of learning with gentle understanding. These moments are examples of people's best nature, becoming teachers, helpers, and friends as they engage across all sorts of social and age boundaries to guide, show, and encourage learning. Somehow these same actions and attitudes are just not so commonly seen when adults interact with one another.

Children do new things at an incredible rate, experiencing and learning as far as their capacity will take them, often to the point of exhaustion. Their willingness to explore newness is extraordinary. The young child's insatiable appetite to learn with absolute abandon is more rarely found in an adult population and someone like that might even be described as atypical, eccentric, or even odd. There are good reasons for adults to exhibit reservation, and certainly times when it is appropriate, but also it is all too common to find the tendency toward restriction and conformity in our learning and in how we approach the various tasks we encounter everyday.

Formal instructional learning is useful, as a manual or textbook can explain about something, but experiencing it for oneself as enactive learning gives us something else and it also requires we actively choose to engage and are willing to embrace risk as a part of the process. This is not the sort of risk that endangers or upsets our way of living or ask us to step out with uncalculated rashness, but every time we do something new – enter an unfamiliar setting or meet someone new, there is an element of unknown, and this can present an unseen risk that makes us question what we know, how we fit, and where we are. There is some form of seen risk with every new situation. Some things may not have severe or obvious consequences like the simplicity of timing and navigating travel to a new place or the challenge of successfully pronouncing and using a new word in conversation, whereas there are other tasks that may seem more obviously 'risky' as they can result in obvious, visible damage or largescale humiliation like falling while rock climbing or forgetting a line while reciting Shakespeare in a full theatre. The approach adults take to various types of task tends to be very different than that of children. For example, as adults we may never even begin.

Children seem to have no reservations in openly exploring the possibilities of how their bodies work. We don't realize the openness with which children experiment with the possibilities of their physicality. When learning to walk, toddlers pull themselves up before their muscles can support their weight and falling is an important part of the process. Even when they fall, they do not give up. They continue to reach and stretch and wobble and fall, and sometimes cry, but consistently get back up.

Consider what they actually do to explore phonation – talking. They make sound by expelling breath over the vocal chords to make sound, a process which is not very controlled to begin with. They work through understanding how the muscles of the face and lips are used to form actual words, exploring the feel of the tongue and the oddness with which it and the other facial muscles move and how these muscles work to change aspects of the sound. Children listen to words and catch them as they are heard, and somehow learn how to reliably move muscles and reproduce sounds that are reliable and intelligible. This takes practice. This experimentation happens both alone, sometimes when nobody is watching, in thought and quiet trials, through watching others, and right out in the open when children go for it in real-time, simply having a conversation. The words do not all come out, grammar may be invented, but they use and apply and make it function far before they 'get it right'. A small child continually makes actual attempts to use their skills by engaging in conversation with those around them. This eagerness, the overt exploration, and the willingness to embrace failure as part of learning are all traits that are not so readily found in the adult populations.

Children readily exhibit enactive learning, where they do it for themselves, and jump straight to putting complex skills like walking and talking into practice in real settings well before they are securely learned. They learn out loud; all the processes are visible. This does not mean their learning is more simplistic. In fact they use quite complex cognitive skills to observe and interpret, extrapolating ideas that are not explicitly presented, and imitate for themselves.

Somehow they do also reliably learn to talk and walk. Both of these are skills need recreating in various situations throughout our lives and the outcome of events depends on us being able to use these skills. It is not as if talking could be created once, like building a piece of flat-packed furniture. You can make a bookcase by following the pictorial instructions and not know a thing about carpentry. Somehow simply repeating a phrase to tick the box for the skill of talking wouldn't be sufficient. To an adult the thought of letting go of the manual even for a little bit can be scary. It can feel less certain or guaranteed to produce a specific result.

The awareness and openness to engage with possibility is something to learn from young children and adopting this in our daily lives ignites a real incentive to learn deeply and comprehensively.

Connecting

Children's early ways of learning are quite different compared to how they will be instructed in their future; at the start of life there is no waiting to be told what to do by a teacher, no next page to turn; no workbook or instruction manual. Even if this direction does exist, often they are not aware enough to follow this type of instruction.

Children connect, communicating and negotiating with one another how things work in various situations and the lack of ego in the very young perhaps helps to facilitate an ease of connection in learning. Children explore with one another. Children help one another. In playing there are definitely rules, but children do not see the formal comparison of ranking and grading of one against the other that is so commonly found in our capitalistic, materially driven adult society. The way children approach learning embodies the principles of connectivism (see end note 1): They reach out to connect with one another, and all they come into contact with helps to contribute to the quest for understanding.

A connectivist network is more complex than a wheel or spider web shape with the source of knowledge at the centre and the students on the outside. Instead connectivism is more like a modern city map. To visualize this, start by imagining each person like a player on a board game with control over what they do, they have agency, the ability to direct their own actions, and can initiate whatever next move they choose. As they interact with other people, places, and things they gain experiences and form a network of understanding that is far beyond the classic direct line of knowledge transmitted from teacher to student. There are some direct paths that are quite easy to find and follow, leading from one house in a neighbourhood to another via the sidewalk, and there are other paths that connect more widely, like roads and highways. The possibilities of connection extend beyond physically going anywhere, and move from the 2D of a map to 3D of real space, with wires and cables linking people across the land, under the ocean, and through the air with audio visual signals bouncing into space and back again.

There is no pre-determined script or set curriculum for connectivism, and when individuals reach out to others, they choose and begin to pave their own path. Even if two people take the same path, they will each have a unique experience. No two connections will yield the same results; unlike in institutionalized learning where the aim is to minimalize variance and to create an even experience for all.

With connectivism, the learning is far more like that of the small child in terms of having the onus be on the person to actively seek, as they explore and experience.

As children grow, the way they are taught to engage with tasks changes dramatically from the initial freedom of exploration they enjoyed as they navigated their surroundings, to what becomes an externally driven and directed methodology, as introduced through timetabled subjects in a school day, where they will meet teachers, textbooks, and tests. As adults we are well versed in following instructions and often produce results by going through the motions, from A to B and so on without really thinking, and as a result we learn very little. In essence, sometimes we *do* without learning, whereas children *learn* with doing.

Adults seem to adopt very different learning practices to our childhood selves. The drive and unhampered verve for doing things that seem to come naturally to young children can disappear rather quickly as they enter formal learning settings. Children move from the freedom of play to the rubric of formality and assessed tasks. This can happen even before any actual teaching or 'learning' happens, for example, as soon as students are alphabetized in rows of desks, or lined up and instructed to stand quietly, waiting to be let in or out of a room. Obedience to authority is introduced, order is imposed, and limits are set as the premise for the framework for learning. *Keep your eyes down, on your own paper.*

Institutional learning does however, aim to create uniformity, at least in terms of measurable results. Schools have syllabi, stream students and rank them into various levels, follow national standards, and measure achievement. Years of schooling indoctrinate children into an ethos that aims to pass the test. Quizzes and exams continually remind people how to distinguish, differentiate, and delineate one from another, and test results can dictate what we can or cannot do. Children are surrounded with behavioural 'norms' for learning and social conventions. As they grow their awareness of the world within and around them develops and they gain a greater understanding of themselves and of others. It is natural to compare and notice and question, and although this is certainly reinforced through school and other social situations, somehow this industrialisation and mass centralized approach to learning is seldom challenged.

School and formalized setting do provide many, many good things. The intent here is to raise awareness of how we sometimes allow our thought processes to be dictated instead of initiating them for ourselves. Ideally we would take the best from formal learning settings while maintaining and developing an approach to awareness that allowed for unexpected possibilities. Why do we allow our initial approach to learning to change so radically?

Tests as goals

As we progress through school there are ever increasing forms of measurement. We are syphoned into a system where everything in our lives becomes focused toward external influences, pre-articulated goals, and tangible rewards. There are years of school reports and grades. In some school systems the progression from one year to another, even at the level of pre-school to primary school is celebrated with gowns and hats, mimicking the traditional academic dress when graduating from university. What exactly is being celebrated? People would say it is achievement, and yes, achievement is *worth* celebrating. But what has been achieved and is this in any way understood or communicated in a relevant way or is it an external rehearsal for what lies ahead? The way you get from one year to another is by achieving acceptable grades. This test has been passed and you might get a sticker, or a hat, or some applause. Even without these, you get to go on to the next test.

Very often people study their required courses with the goal of passing the test and not with anything else particularly in mind as a goal or benefit to being there or undertaking anything asked of them. This probably rings true for at least one topic or subject studied in school, whether because the teacher was perceived of as dull or the subject matter was simply not interesting. I certainly remember taking tests simply to pass and then the 'knowledge' was banked in some distant corner of my brain and not used again. I simply passed a test.

Some particular tests seem to dominate years of people's lives and it is very unclear why. Tests measure and tell us *something about…* I know that is an incomplete sentence and does not make sense on its own. Neither do tests. They tell us something about a person, what someone can do or their tendencies at that moment. Tests in themselves are not skills, in fact taking a test is another skill altogether. The stuff of tests is seldom the same as the world-application of what they are testing. This is partly due to the mass enterprise of educating and test giving and taking, and partly because tests are not always constructed in a way that actually tests the skills in question, but the test-taker does not always understand that. This confusion leaves people stranded after they take the test and receive their piece of paper. Still we have tests that are framed as a goal.

Take the SAT test as an example. This Standardized Aptitude Test covers aspects of numerical and literary understanding and is used for entry to American universities. It is a test that takes three hours to complete and it was devised nearly a hundred years ago. I remember taking the test for the first time when I was 11. At the time I thought it was a game. What were my parents thinking putting me in for it then? Teenage students across the globe spend considerable amounts of time and money in preparation for these benchmarking tests, with the hopes of attaining a certain number on this and similar measures. By design the SAT does not follow on from any particular curriculum studied at school and neither does it relate directly to anything to be studied in higher education. It measures.

People work to learn how to be measured. It would sound

silly to ask someone to undertake a course or any preparation at all to stand against the wall to be measured. A measurement captures and communicates in some agreed, uniform way, what something is, where the some*thing* is usually a skill or quality. In this case the SAT measures aptitude for working with numbers and words. Perhaps these measures can be useful, but I have never heard of a teacher mining into the SAT and working to develop practical applications for improving these aptitudes. It is much more something that would interest a psychologist. They certainly might study scores and test processes (as in the process one undertakes) and perhaps write a paper discussing the theory and implications of the scores or methods, but this has little relevance for the everyday teenager taking the test.

What exactly are we aiming for from all the tests? Years and years of 'getting it', but it is not exactly clear what we get if it's about the numbers. McLuhan described society as always looking in the rear view mirror, thinking they are moving forward but looking backwards. Some of that irony seems to fit with the idea of this test. It was made at a time when cars and refrigerators were rare and nylon stockings had not been invented, let alone the television or computer. Tests are useful to measure, but to have the measurement or the score as the goal misses the point of the skills, misses the point of the learning. Measurement is not everything. We can go beyond.

Throughout our formative years we fix our attention, as instructed, on measurable goals as they are presented to us. In a standard education a student will have, at a minimum, over a decade of experience with taking tests. Children have had tests as a constant factor in their lives through childhood and all the way through, until they reach the age of legal adulthood. Lots else besides tests happens in school too, with many varied opportunities introducing people to what can become formative and very valuable, genuine learning moments. Real skills will be introduced and honed and for some they will find new interests in topics they had never encountered before, and these can lead them to pursue a lifetime of meaningful experiences.

School is full of tests though, and the snapshot that is captured through an assessment is a momentary view of whatever skills or abilities are being tested. There are many different tests that people leap to and from, and sometimes they are useful.

People undertake pursuits that involve tests where the end goal is not simply the number or grade they get, but something more. The driving test is a good example. Interestingly this is not one of the things uniformly taught in school and the approach to driving is quite different from that of other subjects. Many young people choose to learn to drive, and when they choose it, they are aware that they need to not only understand the concepts involved, but they will have to actively demonstrate their new skills in a holistic way. The skills, theory, and ability to manage multiple unforeseen inputs is put into practice in a real-time, real-life variable, unpredictable situation when the student sits in the car with an examiner to actually drive the car on the road, in real traffic for their test.

Once someone does pass and gets their driving license, there will definitely be a moment of celebration in recognition of the achievement, the huge whoop and obligatory photo to share with friends and family, but that is not the end. There is no sense of having done that subject and closing a book, as there often is with the end of other courses. This celebration is not focused on the hindsight of having learned to drive or even on the details of the grade received, but even without prompting people have vision. That is a useful test and interestingly, nobody has to *tell* the person who passes their test that they now have possibilities that can be exercised with this newly confirmed skill. There is something about the way we approach this task and the wider understanding that sits outside the way other formal exams are regarded. Once that license is in hand, that person's eye is already cast forward onto what can be practically done with this success. Their focus lies on what possibilities literally lie over the horizon and how to get there. From the point of achieving a driving license onward, people tend to continue to use and develop the skills they learned. The application of the skill is then fitted into daily life and facilitates our doing any number of other things. It is clear to see how passing this test is useful and instead of the test being the goal, people speak of using these skills in the future as the goal.

When done is done and we shut the door to awareness all by ourselves:

The school graduation ceremony does in fact represent an end. That chapter of life and the learning that took place there is over. There is bound to be at least one subject that people were made to learn that they will not willingly touch in the foreseeable future, and certainly not the way it was presented. For me this subject was history. I barely made it through high school history. I couldn't see the point of memorising the dates and lists of who did what where and when. For me it didn't have any relevance to my teenage life. That is not to say that learning history was not worthwhile. In fact learning what came before you is one of the very most important things there is. It teaches us to observe and gives us a perspective beyond what we ourselves can see now, beyond where we live and who we know now. It gives us a chance to watch how lives played out and consider decisions people made and the consequences they faced. The study of history gives us foresight that normally only hindsight, gained through experiences over time, can give. Unfortunately I could not see any of that from my segmented, multiple choice, summer-school high school class' introduction to the dim and distant past where I accessed my short-term memory to memorise facts about places I had never been to about people who seemingly had no connection to me. When I was done and had ticked the boxes required for that class, I switched off simply because I could. Heck, I passed the test, was done, and even had a piece of paper to prove I was done fair and square.

What I actually did was to shut a metaphorical door right in my face, and I did this by choice. I earned the pass required by law in high school history (even if it was in summer school) and nobody was going to make me learn anything else ever. That's what I thought and that is what I chose.

I was very wrong.

This was not the only path and years later I found myself, unbeknownst to me, learning by the bucketful. I stumbled upon a museum a few miles from where I lived which was called an 'open air museum'. It was on a hill surrounded by sheep and farmland, and old buildings were transported there, stone by stone, and rebuilt using the traditional methods that would have been employed at the time of their original construction. It contained houses from every century back to the 1400s, just dotted across the grassy hillside. The museum had dedicated volunteers who studied how people did things in the past and they relayed this by telling stories, making the crafts, preserving the food, grinding the grain and making the bread in the open fire oven, and by demonstrating how the original inhabitants of these houses would have lived. I would walk with my young children, and the volunteers would talk with me when I asked questions:

In the centre of the big main room of the Bayleaf Farmstead, dating from the mid 15th Century, a volunteer tended the fire. We talked as I warmed by the fire, small child on my back, and watched the smoke rise up to the small open holes in the corners of the roof and the slats in the wall, where centuries later there would be glass. He pointed to a clay dome on the ground by the side of the fire and asked if I knew what it was. No, I replied and looked curiously at him. He said its name was French and it related to another word. It was a couvre feu, which means 'cover the fire'. He asked what other word sounded like couvre feu, and gave me a hint by asking me to think of when people might cover a fire? I was interested. He explained that in the late 1400's and early 1500s there was certainly no electricity and few ordinary people had any way beside the sun to tell the time. When winter came it got dark early and it could be difficult to know when the hours in the afternoon melted into evening. The *curfew* was when someone in the town or village rang a bell to let people know it was time to cover the fire and turn in for the night. Now that was history and it was useful and I loved it. I sought stories about the stones, the animals, the food, the clothes, and continued to seek stories from the people with whom I came into contact in my life. This was a living history and went far beyond any test. There is nothing multiple choice about this, no tests, just life.

I was so lucky to stumble onto this museum and strike up that initial conversation. Mostly, when we are finished doing the learning someone else requires of us and we get that piece of paper saying we have indeed finished, even though the idea is that we have finished that measurable task instead of implying we have achieved Parnassus, we very happily choose to switch off. It is so easy to shut the door to awareness because of the confusing finality with which tasks and tests are presented to us. It is like we willingly turn off the lights in our brains without realising what we are doing, or rather what we are stopping ourselves from doing.

The learning I found at the museum was magic because I didn't know it was happening. Had someone told me I was going to learn about history I would have said no, because I disliked it so much in school. The fact that I was learning truly caught me by surprise and it wasn't until now, writing this, that I realized the extent to which I was learning. My interest in history is actually intense, and I actually pursue it every day.

Picture of assessment

When you look at a picture, what do you see?

With any given picture there will be some aspects of the situation that can be described by looking at it, and there will be other information that is missing completely. A snapshot is a single view and does not necessarily represent an enduring disposition or set of qualities about that person. Even though it does not tell the whole story, it is one view of a multifaceted set of circumstances and is often viewed as a whole.

Similarly when we accomplish something, whether we chose it or it was required by someone of us, the idea of being finished can be quite a release. In the picture above, I had ridden from London to Brighton and I was done. Really done. I couldn't do it again now, simply because that was a moment, the achievement was then, but it is not something that remains constant still now. The understanding that learning is somehow accomplished and remains forever, without need for further attention is counter-intuitive but not at all uncommon.

The way ideas are presented to us and we understand them can give us a limited view of ourselves, and this includes the concept of 'having learned' something. Learning is good. It is great in fact, but this is quite a simplistic, fixed understanding that rather resembles looking at the snapshot and thinking it shows the whole story. One important thing that is missing is an ongoing sense of reflection on process, both during and after it happens, and on the experience gained to get to the point of being able to recognize learning has been achieved.

The brain and perception

Within our physical selves we have wonderful machinery that allows us to take in the world around us. Our senses are astonishing, and the degree to which we use them is very small compared to their potential. How sensitive are the delicate fingertips of a person who reads the small dots of Braille, the ears that guide the calloused fingers of the violinist, the perception of solidity that the rock climber feels, the taste of a triggered memory? – I'm thinking now of distant summer strawberries, warmed in the sun, and the vivid sensation of biting into the fruit, feeling the juice run down the side of my hand, the taste of tang and sweetness, and smell that uniquely strawberry smell comes flooding through my mind's eye. I get everything but a full tummy from that.

This sort of musing is hardly entertained in everyday life, and might be thought of as reserved purely for the creatives. We all can perceive more fully than we know, (see end note 2) however if our senses and faculties work, we tend to use them very little and progress along a path of least resistance, often in a learned and familiar pattern. There are so many demands placed on people every day to get on and *do* daily life, that it seems there is hardly time or energy left to notice anything beyond what we need to get the task at hand done.

Test this for yourself and look at the people around you.

It is especially easy to see when people are getting places. Sometimes when travelling there is a need to concentrate on carrying out a task, like driving a car. Have you noticed how commuters look on the train? This can be 'dead time' as it must be endured to get from A to B, but the traveller is not required to actively take part in the process of making the train go – they are a passenger. I notice these people when spending the day in London or visiting another city abroad. It is often a strange and almost inhuman experience with silent bodies sitting and standing quietly, very close together, but acting as if alone. Most eyes are down or half shut as if to minimize the possibility of being noticed and keep out external glances. If any eyes are looking out they tend to be either fixed on reading something or glazed and indistinct. It is unusual to make actual contact with someone and it would be uncharacteristic and possibly surprising behaviour. This seems more than strange, and verging on unnatural. That is not to say it is not *normal*; it is completely normal behaviour in our society, but it is not natural. The people who do continue to make contact despite this morgue of a situation are the children. They still follow their instincts to reach out, sense, and take in. Odd how as we grow, we recoil. Our senses are so rich, however, unfortunately it is all too common that people hardly know what is possible until they *must*.

When something is taken from us, we find another way. For example, if sight is taken we learn to use the other senses more attentively. When I lived with my in-laws, they had a visit from the piano tuner who was blind. Upon arriving for his first visit, he was welcomed into the house and he asked if he could wash his hands before beginning work on their piano. My mother-in-law offered to show him to the bathroom, but he declined. He said he didn't need guidance as he could smell the hand soap. What an awakening it was to realize that something as simple as the smell of soap existed and could be meaningful, and the balance of what one person perceives is not somehow finite or anywhere close to the same as what another experiences, even in the same place and time. Our faculties allow for such richness, if we entertain it.

"Millions of items of the outward order are present to my senses which never properly enter my experience. Why? Because they have no *interest* for me. *My experience is what I agree to attend to.* Only those items which I notice shape my mind – without selective interest, experience is an utter chaos." (James, Principles I, p. 402)

The mechanics of perception come before considering or attending to interest, intent, and making meaning from experience. As a musician I have been trained to listen. This was not a perception I previously used to the extent I do now. The mechanism existed, but it was neither honed, nor was I aware or skilled in using it.

Sound exists and our ears hear. That short sentence stands alone because unlike our eyes that we can shut or our hands that we can put in our pockets, we cannot stop hearing as long as our ears work. Sounds bombard from every direction at all times of day and night and perhaps the way in which we choose or adapt is most obvious with hearing. The person who lives near an air field hardly notices the planes, the noise inside a car is tolerated without question, and the hum of the electric appliances and lights in houses and offices somehow fades away. There are mechanisms by which we subconsciously decide what is most important on an almost animal level, stemming from days where sound signalled danger. There are still sounds that are practically hard-wired to create a reaction in humans like sudden loud sounds. Even heard in a bustling soundscape, the piercing cry of an infant is one least likely to go unnoticed or to be filtered out as unimportant.

Seeing

The visual field is very different to auditory field. Although we are surrounded by sound every moment of our lives, we can quite easily shut out vision. The only ways to shut off sound are shown to us by infants where they either drown out the stimulus of sound by being louder (!) or literally turn themselves off – by relinquishing control of their consciousness and going to sleep. These are our only practical ways to shut off sound. Even in an anechoic chamber there is the sound of our bodies working. The pumping heart and rushing blood in veins becomes deafeningly loud. When we are overwhelmed by vision, we can control it far more easily by simply shutting our eyes.

Even beyond control of what we see, we have limits to what we can take in. Unlike sound, our vision is not 360º, it is in fact far less. You can test this for yourself. Hold your arms open wide, one stretched to the left and one to the right. If you look straight ahead, you will not be able to see your hands. We cannot see 180º. That is only half of what surrounds us. It takes focused, directed attention to see. Besides not seeing all around us in the same way that we hear, our eyes also have an even more limited central focus for vision.

The slice of the world in front of us where we can see most clearly, with accurate colors and greatest detail is only about an 8% window. In practical terms that is a really narrow slit. If you imagine the face of an analogue clock on the wall, the distance from 12 to 3 is 90º, and that means the distance between each of the numbers is 30º. Half of that is 15º and half of that is just under 8º. So ¼ of the distance between two numbers on a clock face is the range that our eyes are able to see the world with clarity, focus, and color. Astonishingly, there are fewer receptors (called rods) in the eye for detecting what we see on the periphery, with far less clarity and far less color. That does not mean we cannot see, but there is a lot of interpretative data that goes into making the 'full picture' of what we see.

Medical practitioners can explain aspects of how we work, for example when people read the eye stops specifically on each word and then move on. The way we look at words in that tiny window of clear view is clever and complex; there is a greater window of attention leaning ahead of the words. We anticipate, so if reading left to right the eye looks a bit further to the right. We direct our sight to find the detail.

One experiment carried out by neuroscientists Cohen and Rubenstein (2019) demonstrated the astonishing nature of how little we do see on the edges. People were shown an image and asked one of two simple questions: Did it have a face? or Was it an indoor or outdoor scene? This encouraged people to focus on the centre of the image and they were shown a series of images. They saw ten normal images and on the eleventh image, there was something drastically different. Only that central focus area, the 8% slice of the image was kept as normal and the rest was either in black and white or the colors were completely altered from reality. For example one image showed a swimmer and the water outside the central 8% was bright pink. Another image showed the grass of a sports stadium for the majority of the image to be luminous purple. These changes would be instantly noticed if seeing the whole picture. In the experiment the limit of what could be seen at once was tested and people only had a fraction of a second to actually 'see' the image. Over 75% of people did not notice *anything at all* wrong with the drastically altered image. The experiment did not conclude that we are stupid or color blind, but that we need time to direct our attention to fill in the gaps (see end note 3 for full article and further reading).

To see, and take in what is in front of us, we do not simply open our eyes and look. Our eyes undertake patterns of darting back and forth to glimpse beyond straight ahead and relay detail back to the brain. Our brains fill in the detail there and it is only when we gather new information for some reason, that we update and redefine what is on the edges. Otherwise it is rather like an old hand drawn cartoon where only the main character in the centre of the screen moves and the back is a stock image. Noticing different pieces of the world around us gives the brain clues from which we can extrapolate all sorts of useful information, telling us of a possible function of another useful object in the field of view, like whether we can sit on a chair (see end note 4), or noticing specifics about faces and the emotions they convey. All of this happens when we begin to pay attention, to notice and widen our focus and what is around us takes on new meaning. Otherwise we stick to *seeing* that narrow window and what is on the periphery really could be anything, whether trivial details or life changing opportunities. It would just pass us by and we would never know it was there at all. When we focus with our eyes, we see can see the details around the edges and widen our experience. This is a challenge and if we are to keep aware, it takes more than a blink or cursory glance. This is an active way of being.

When we stop looking

There are ways to stop looking at what is around us, from literally withdrawing into the world of sleep to covering our eyes so we do not have to see a particular scene before us. These are physical ways to stop looking, but we also are very used to accepting and imposing limits on ourselves that have the impact of blinders on a horse, except unlike the horse wearing its head gear, we don't even know these boundaries and barriers exist because they are not physical at all. There is a wonderfully powerful limitation presented to and upon us by our thoughts and beliefs, and this can be illustrated by the power we grant to everyday words and phrases. Here I should clarify what I mean by beliefs: I do not mean religious beliefs, but the psychological understanding of what you know and accept to be true. For example if you see a chair there will be certain assumptions you make about it. *That chair is sturdy and can comfortably hold my weight. I can sit on it.* The same types of judgements are made about the properties of things and the relationships of people and even about our own capabilities. It is our internal understandings of these that I refer to as our beliefs. Self-efficacy is the psychological belief about our personal capability to do specific tasks, and this will be very central in the chapters to come.

There is so much limitation in commonly used words and phrases that is unknowingly tolerated and perpetuated. Think back to the child who could not understand the concepts of private and public thought as they attempt the 'what hand is it in' game. In life, probably at school, some encouraging adult will ask, 'What do you want to be when you grow up?' Perhaps they will be told encouragingly, 'Ah you can be anything at all!' The intention in this sentiment is liberating if left as an open-ended question to ignite dreams and be a catalyst for future vision. That thought is lovely. However, generally a reply is expected, and this is when the problems start.

How do you decide what to become? Well this is the trick in the question. It is liberating to ask the open-ended question 'what would you like?', but as soon as an answer is required and we put a name to the 'what', everything changes. Doors can be opened and shut with seemingly immovable limitations. Where is the limit in declaring what you might want to be? The problem is in the whole situation. In order to choose anything to be, to put a name to it, someone has to already know the name of what they are about to choose. It is impossible to declare what you want if it is unknown to you or has not yet been invented. Someone could truly want to become President, or become a pilot, or an artist, or a surgeon, and these are wonderful goals, but the choices someone has are limited by the words in their vocabulary. To answer the question, they draw from the deck of cards which is their own understanding and play an answer they already know. How can the child answer in any effective way? (and would they want to?)

These problems stem from a lack of perspective and understanding. The person asking has a view like standing on top of a mountain, having seen a lifetime of possibilities they either realized or missed. They have the benefit of hindsight and knowing their past as well as a societal past of decades gone by, where, even in recent history many different people, whether because of gender, color, wealth, or some other reason, were not allowed to entertain the idea of becoming 'what they wanted'.

The question is not all bad. We do not need to know the answer; we need to be given permission (and guidance) to dream. When that permission is granted, something happens. Let me put it in a positive light and explain with a story. Imagine a class of children at their desks in school. There is a paper on the desk with that question on it, and yes, I have rephrased it slightly: 'What do you want to become?' The children instinctively reach for their pencils, but the teacher stops them, saying, 'There is not an answer. The only answer is you. As you grow you will learn, developing special skills and qualities, but you will never be anything other than you. You will not turn into a tree or a building. The job or role you have in life will be a way for you to use the things you do best, hopefully for good. You will not become the job, but will still be you. Instead of listing the name of a job, can you list the things you might like to do. Then you can learn to look for ways of making that happen.'

Looking back at the question, we find even more limitation in the second half of that simple question. It is supposed to be aspirational to ask a child what they want to be when you grow up, but the whole concept of 'grown up' is full of limitation, and for someone who has reached adulthood, thinking about what you want to be and whether or not you 'got there' can be anything but aspirational. Is grown up a place we get to or a time of life, or the end of something? Maybe it is like graduation. Does that imply that when people arrive at being grown up that they are done? If something is done, then that implies it has finished and whoever is doing it is likely to not be doing it any longer. So following that argument, we grow, and then we stop? That is so very counterproductive and just so wrong. This is not the only phrase associated with adulthood that implies finality. Maybe they're 'over the hill'. What a dire phrase, especially considering that relates to being 40, which is approximately half of the modern lifespan. In life nobody is done at a certain age. Some external arbitrary label should not define your capabilities. If you wake up in the morning, you are not finished. On a basic level you can fill in the blank and see what happens if you stop. If you stop exercising your body will atrophy. (that's a polite way of saying your muscles will go to mush.) If you stop eating or breathing, you will die. That is harsh, but true. If you stop seeing you go blind. If you stop learning you do not maintain your brains, they too fade just like memories. Status quo is not achieved by stopping. Anyone who has lost weight will tell you that once they reach their goal it is not over, as maintenance takes work. Because of the nature of life, we exist in time and space, and certainly the way we experience it, time keeps moving forward. Life is growth and growth requires change, and with awareness - which we can choose and develop - comes learning. When people stop, their vision narrows and both perception and understanding of the possibilities around them fade too.

If there is no door to see, how can people say yes and walk through it?

Stop, Look, and Listen!

Learning awareness starts with our basic functionality: how you move physically in time and space. If we all direct ourselves whichever ways we want to go, with no consideration of others, there will be collisions. There was a kiddie road safety programme for pre-schoolers near my elementary school where they made a mock-up of a little town (it must have been on a playground) and everyone got to go round on trikes and scooters and things. There were roads and stop signs and traffic lights and pedestrian crossings. Some were really lucky and got one of the sought after big-wheels bikes, which was a particular plastic pedal-trike where the seat was really low to the ground and your feet were out front, turning a rather large single, front wheel. If you haven't seen one, it can be described as a mix between a recumbent trike and a Harley Davidson for 3 year olds. It was super cool and if you pedalled hard, you could even spin the front wheel. I seem to remember collisions were not uncommon with the giant plastic trikes, and they were pretty harmless most of the time.

Beside the fun bikes, all the children in the programme were learning about awareness through the popular phrase: **Stop, Look, and Listen!** It was good advice then and still is today, even with the introduction of electric cars on the roads where there is a need to do far more looking rather than relying on hearing the roar of an engine. Those words are still useful for us as a lesson in everyday awareness. With something like driving, it is clear what the rules are and how people are supposed to behave. As a result, accidents can be avoided. In life there are many more undefined and unexpected factors, and unplanned bumps with people definitely gets less fun as life goes on. We are already quite skilled at navigating the expected obstacles around us. Generally we think of finding our path as avoiding the crashes, but it is also about opportunities. It is tricky to *see* an opportunity if you neither expect it nor know what it might look like. It can be as simple as literally seeing in a new light. The thing to cultivate is a heightened awareness that allows for slight surprises.

If we are forced to look through a new lens the 'new light' experience can be facilitated. I have never been in a sensory deprivation tank, but I have been in an anechoic chamber at the Harley Street Ear Clinic when I had my hearing tested and got fitted ear plugs. The anechoic chamber creates a quiet by removing all outside sound. It was not quite silent, as in with no sound at all, because you could hear your own body working. I could hear the sound of my blood flowing. That was strange, but I don't think I really had any sort of a-ha moment there. I knew what was going to happen and there you go. Having an induced silence was not the experience that really impacted me. Another, less drastic situation that surprised me more and changed the way I understood my own awareness was scuba diving.

Scuba stands for 'Self-Contained Under Water Breathing Apparatus' and it takes us under the water for extended lengths of time. Most people have experienced the sensation of being under water, specifically of having both ears under the water, in either a swimming pool or a bathtub. It sounds different. You can still hear, but sound is distorted. If you are under water for any length of time you will start to listen differently. Once you go below the water's surface when scuba diving there are very few sounds beside that of your own breathing. It takes the form of a deep raspy inhale through the regulator (mouth piece) and a smooth sound of bubbles with the exhale. This experience of sound was decidedly different to the anechoic chamber because I could *control* my breathing, and I heard it. The speed or calm of my breath was the one thing at the forefront of my attention and I was very aware of how I interacted with and reacted to my surroundings. Completely removing one sense did not make me more aware but hearing only certain sounds certainly did.

There was something else down there that further focused my awareness in a surprisingly dramatic way. It was the water itself. When underwater we feel the density and thickness of what surrounds us, the water, in a very different way to the everyday feeling of air. Air is just there, and it goes unnoticed like it's nothing, but in the water I was aware of how I moved through it and I was aware of its resistance to me. I could sense the physical space between me and wherever I was going. It was vast and different to looking at a mountain on land, I was not focused on a thing I could already see, instead I experienced the weight of the water everywhere, all over my body in every motion. There was an eternity of thick nothing surrounding me, filled only by the sound of my breathing. Being confronted with the space that would normally go unnoticed if it was air made me aware of my size and the enormity of everything. Floating in the middle of the water, I was keenly aware of being a drop in the ocean, and for a moment I understood something about the breadth of the world and how we as people exist within it.

My awareness under the water was completely unexpected. I was not looking for a revelation. Actually I was looking for some old boat or other, but there was enough of a gap between what I expected and what I knew that *something else* could slip in to my perception. I held onto that feeling and when I got back on the land and felt the wind, I breathed easy. Instead of having the feeling of being lost in the ocean, I felt the strength in my motions when moving through the air. That woke the need to realize, pay attention, and look for things beyond what happened to fall on my doorstep.

CHAPTER TWO
Life's Maze

The other evening as I climbed into bed, I did the very usual thing of reaching down and toward the wall for my phone's charging cable. As I plugged it in a reminder flashed up on the screen asking if I'd like to set an alarm for 6:15 am.   I thought, *'What?!. 6:15? No way do I want an alarm then.'* Even though I had gotten up at 6:15 every day that week, after being made aware of that pattern by seeing it there in front of me, I took the choice not to set an alarm. How much of our lives can be reduced to a routine like predicting the weather mid-way through a season, where tomorrow's weather is most likely to be similar to how it was today? The variation from yesterday to today, and then onward to tomorrow tends to be minimal. Often unbeknown to us the same is true for many aspects of our lives. Cue the bridge lyrics by Paul McCartney in the song "A day in the life" by The Beatles. If you don't know them, they describe the monotonous morning routine involving stumbling out of bed, a coffee, and getting to work in a daze.

From our very beginning expectations are set out, given, and imposed on us throughout everyday life, at home, in education, socially, and in our careers. There are rules and parameters present that can either feel like a restraint or be an affirming way to measure success and even allow us freedom across all aspects of life. There is no textbook or prescription for life, no perfect anything, yet there are all sorts of assumptions and stipulations on how people are supposed to be, whether about defining or understanding what constitutes a good job or a good parent, or even how someone should look or speak. Even for the most stalwart of person, this can really put a damper on the overall sense of *yes* – that sense of agency, belief, and personal drive - in life.

The opportunity not (initially) taken

(Pastels on construction paper, Catherine Ritchie, age 9)

As a child I remember being told *be a good girl now, and do what you're told.* As people we are always learning and figuring out what is around us, and even as small people we are very quick to understand people, places, and ways that either are acceptable or not. When people speak to young children, they often attempt to use simple clear language: Be *nice* to the doggy. These directives teach us many things, but the polar opposites of the words yes (no) or good (bad) may not always fit neatly into boxes without explanations. Thinking and asking *why* is necessary so we can understand the context and confirm or question and change our assumptions.

My daughter was seven years old when her little brother was born, and she shared a bedroom with him for several years. When he was just about a year old they were quietly playing in their bedroom, each occupied at separate ends of the room. She was at her desk reading and he was doing something – playing with a soft toy, or so I thought. Suddenly she shouted to me, absolutely furious, saying, 'MUMMY HE'S DRAWN ON MY WALL!' I came and she pointed to the light green scribbles at toddler-height on the white wall. I looked at the wall, sighed, looked back at her, and in earnest asked, *'Well, are you going to draw something better?'*

This was absolutely not the answer she was expecting and at first looked at me with disbelief, still raging at her brother, and then she slowly realized I was not kidding at all. *'What?? But he's…'* she tried. *Why not?* I told her quite plainly, not asking, but telling, and explained, *'He drew on your wall and it is not very good. It is a scribble.'* It was unintentional, and it would be very different if she intentionally did actually draw on the wall. I was completely sure she could think up something better, and given permission and the possibility, she did. She sat there for a while and by the afternoon had begun to draw on that blank canvas of a wall. In a few weeks it was covered with intricate nature scenes and she has kept drawing ever since.

I am not suggesting anyone has or should have free license to draw on whatever wall is nearest. However, the concept that any *thing* only has a fixed use and deviation is inherently wrong is not a helpful outlook. What it says on the tin may be one use, but what else can it be used for, and why? A friend used the idea of challenging our unseen assumptions as an activity to encourage thinking and discussion in groups. He gave people a typical everyday object – a paper cup or a fork or a paperclip, and asking the question, *'Can you come up with 100 uses for this?'* At first people tend to be stumped because the object is already defined by its most common use. It's a cup. Well yes, but you can do other things with it. You could also take out the bottom of the cup and make it into a pretend telescope, you can use it as a shape to make sandcastles, or a cookie cutter, or as a building brick in a cup tower, or add a piece of string and make it into a children's telephone... You get the idea? They learn to think wider by asking how can the form, the materials, the shape, the structure be useful in other ways beside the most common use? It's just like seeing a wall differently and using it as a canvas.

My reply served as a complete shift in perception for my daughter. She was initially completely fixated on what her brother did, finger-pointing toward him, and had not at all entertained what she would do about it. What she expected from me was to cast blame and tell her brother something along the lines of, *'you shouldn't do that,'* but instead I asked her to focus on what *she could do*. It was important to acknowledge him and what he did, and I did take the pen out of his hand, but the positive focus of the possibility of moving forward provided a different direction for the situation.

There are reasons we don't draw on the walls inside our houses. This could be to avoid the poor aesthetic of something perhaps not done by an artist, the idea of permanence, or simply because paper is convenient and we don't need a whole wall. Where there is a need and we are allowed to explore by using creative open thinking, this is how new ideas become inventions. The parameters defined by the needs help to shape what is created. At some point in history, someone must have thought that putting notes on the wall was better than using only paper on a desk, perhaps in a meeting where multiple people needed to see the notes at once. For showing ideas in this way we have chalk boards, and to lessen the dust and the ease of changing the visible text, these became dry erase boards. Using a physical board still required people to be in the room, and that limits the pool of minds that can be present in the space. With the invention of computers and tablets, which effectively allow electronic paper, people across the world can *see* in real time and take part in a discussion, adding their own ideas across the ether. If we can identify what we want to do in a situation, then we can entertain the possibility of how, by allowing ourselves to consider differently. We can adapt and invent uses for things and materials depending on the purpose and circumstance, to create a functionality that serves the needs we have at the time.

In a maze?

In 1948, Tolman, a behavioural psychologist, published experiments studying how rats think to show how they coped with the challenge of navigating their physical surroundings and how a goal might influence them. At the time animals were thought to be pretty straightforward in terms of their decision making processes. Tolman wanted to see if rats could learn to figure out the way through a maze. Of course they did find their way to the exit, and then they were either simply taken out of the maze by a researcher or found the reward of some food. After the rats who just walked through to the end (without the lure of food) were taken out of the maze, they would be put back in their cages without any reward at all. The rats who got food at the end of the maze sniffed around the corners and figured out how to zip through far more quickly than the others who didn't really have a specific goal. A big finding was that the rats used clues from their understanding of their environment to figure out and mentally map the maze, but the food motivated them to achieve that goal faster. The understanding at the time was that people were thought to follow quite similar thought processes to these rats. Now we understand that humans have far more complex thought and learning processes, but I wonder how many aspects of our everyday life today are similar to that study of rats wandering through a maze over 70 years ago?

Jobs across society include monotonous and repetitive tasks, that's inescapable. Every-day things from moving items from one place to another- whether to a shelf, drawer, or a building, entering figures in books or computers, even the daily commute are just things we do. In some jobs there are the sort of tasks that pile up, one after the other. Especially when deadlines are involved, we can feel vaulted from one task to the next. When this feeling spills over into life it can be like pushing the pencil with very little thought from one number to another in a connect the dots puzzle or dabbing water on all the number 3s in a paint by numbers picture. You go there and do it because that's what it says to do. Sometimes when carrying out tasks we are contributing our part to something wonderful or creative, but other times there may be little sense of awareness or purpose in what we're doing, being driven by the 'have to' or 'they said' or by the pay check at the end of the week or month can feel quite similar to the experience of Tolman's rats, only we're running through life and not a maze.

The reward of arriving somewhere, whether a pay check or some other marker, can create an illusion of appearing clever or to have won. We've done it! - sniffed around the corners, navigated the tunnels and passageways and found the reward. It can become a perpetual cycle. This isn't necessarily an achievement, but can be made to look like a reward or something we *should* do, and it keeps us running as if on a treadmill. Some people carry on, head down, to the extent where months turn into years, and sometimes we can forget why or what and somehow get lost in that maze. The need or desire to get out is kept at bay as long as there is something instantly pleasing – food, technology, some reward to reassure us and keep us going when approaching what could look like an exit.

In life people aren't literally in a maze, and few jobs or

pursuits are actually quite so stringent or dreary, but no matter how wonderful our life pursuits, there will be mundane tasks. We walk around corners and go through plenty of doors, both real and metaphorical, every day in life and work settings, and it is entirely possible that we hardly notice or see them. In this sense, an unseen maze can engulf many of us in aspects of our everyday lives.

Living in a modern world we are bound by time, tied to jobs, and sometimes it can seem like we are part of a big machine - 'just another brick in the wall' as Pink Floyd sang. We don't need to work in the same way as people once did, to tend the land, hunt, or make the cloth for our clothes, but we are still driven by jobs and careers, and finding time for ourselves can be a hurdle. Time has long been interwoven with the idea of work, and not simply a measure of the sun's passage in the sky. The sun measured the working day in Egyptian society. In more recent times where peasants were made to work, time was described in terms of tasks - two shakes of a lamb's tail or the cooking time of a particular food - rather than being measured by the sun or a mechanical clock. The notion of a clock dictating work-time became a reality for English factory workers in the late 1700s. A water-driven clock was used in Derbyshire that was regulated by the quality and speed of worker's labour, and not the even ticking of time as we know it. The time you owed your employer did not end with a certain number of hours or sundown, but when you completed your quota. Daily grind? Indeed. If the clock didn't read the right quantity of work-time you were not done for the day. This sounds horrendous, but there are still huge shadows in the modern way of thinking and living that hang over us from these practices. Day in and day out we clock in and work. Waiting for the weekend? Waiting for Godot? Or just running round the maze?

It is a myth though that our society is fixed, unchangeable, and that we are trapped within it. Even while living within it, we can challenge the concept of being a cog, a brick, or being stuck like a rat in a maze. The bottom line is we aren't crawling in a maze and in many ways we can just get up, look over the walls, and walk out.

Identifying the habits of life

Limits and limiters

In life various processes, products, and prospects are presented to us as a *fait accompli*, as something already established that we simply have to deal with. But is that really so? Here's a very simple example that has no ideological, cultural, or even religious bearing, but is just one of those things that has probably never crossed your mind before. I was driving, and my son was in the car with me. The car is a hybrid so sometimes it runs off electricity and we like to watch the digital record of how many miles we get per gallon. We stopped to fill the tank, and my son wanted to reset the trip monitor so we could measure this tank as compared to our mileage from the last tank. I said of course, and he pressed the button. As we drove off, the car used electricity and the monitor read 99.99 miles per gallon. My son thought this was pretty cool and asked if he could update it again quickly while it was still running on electricity so we would have an awesome record for the 'trip'.

Then he asked, *'Why does it say 99.99?'*, and added quickly, *'Why doesn't it say 999,999.99? It's not using any petrol at all, so shouldn't it be a million miles to the gallon?'*

He was so right. Why does it say 99? Is the 'goal' 100? It's not a percent. 100 is nowhere near the actual mileage the car gets (unfortunately) so it is not even a realistic approximation of a limit. I later told this story to an adult student of mine who shrugged her shoulders and said we are just conditioned that way. Yes, there are so many products and activities that are presented as you *need* this or you *must do* this, but is that really true? When we allow things or tasks to be dictated or limited, without giving them due consideration, we are in danger of falling into habitual behaviours. The repeated processes we undertake everyday can be done with little or no active thought or awareness, almost on automatic pilot. When something becomes habit, it is woven into the fabric of your life, and if that weave has lots of habits, those patterns can be our defining features. Convention and habit can be good, but often this is not the case. *Doing*, action, needs thought. In learning there are processes of iterative thought, before, during, and after action, and for any growth to take place, some change is necessary. Following convention or expectation is not necessary. It may help you to progress to a goal, but if the aspect of deliberate choice and thinking is missing then habit won't take you far and action will be superficial. Awareness and thinking equip us to make choices. Through choices there can be strategic thinking, and this leads to a meta awareness of our mental processes.

One single voice

One voice can make a difference in small and big ways, and it doesn't have to be by doing something larger than life. With the insight to see differently, outside that societal maze, and the conviction of self-belief to carry out a task, even the smallest acts can begin to shift the way we see ourselves in the world.

There was man called F.M. Alexander, who was an

Australian Shakespearean actor living at the turn of the 1900s who had voice problems. Initially these involved projection and then they developed into a painful condition where he couldn't speak at all on stage. He sought medical advice and doctors found nothing physically wrong with him. Through careful self-observation he realized he developed so much habitual tension in his body that he physically prevented himself from producing sound on stage. He did learn to relax, and he also learned just how damaging built-up habits could be, and he set out to devise steps to undo the tension blocking his voice and his career as an actor. These steps became the basis for a popular method for understanding and practising the release of physical tension and is now known as 'Alexander Technique'. A main premise of the Alexander Technique is to inhibit bad habits of motion in the body and retrain yourself with good habits. Basically, before undertaking an action like sitting or standing, you mentally say STOP and then notice, think, and act in a deliberate way. There are mantras about releasing tension from muscles so your body, the spine and neck in particular, can be free. The conscientious practice of awareness and the active inhibition of the negative behaviour makes a dramatic difference to those everyday activities that would otherwise be on autopilot. Any change of habit is a huge challenge, and there are so many things that we do without any awareness at all, while our bodies and minds are so good at adaptive behaviours to mask something that might be having a momentary marginally negative impact on us. Especially when we are not aware of them, these moments add up to become habits instead of choices. In Alexander Technique, as the number of times we pause before doing and think mount to outweigh the role of automatic pilot in our lives, we begin to notice we can stand up that little bit taller and just be a bit more free.

It is important to reflect and ask whose voice do we privilege? Is it the media through polished ads on billboards, tv shows, or the person who shouts loudest on social platforms? Do we recognize and listen to our own voice? The world moves so fast whether the news or in the fire hose of online media, and people are presented life and its choices in a way that looks ready-for-consumption, like all we need to do is pick up the relevant pieces and they slot into place for us, just as they're supposed to. Our lives aren't flat-packed bookcases. There is no supposed to. Nobody else has lived your life and nobody else knows what you could do for yourself or for the world.

Everyday stuff

Daily tasks that we do without conscious consideration can still be carried out with conviction. Behind every action is belief. At some point we decided that we are perfectly capable of doing certain things, and when they become routine the internal decision making process becomes nearly undetectable. We do these tasks with complete certainty and without fear of failure or any negative repercussions. For example, in the morning when you get your breakfast there is unlikely to be real worry of dropping the cereal bowl on the floor or spilling everywhere, and it would be laughable to suggest you might genuinely fear squirting toothpaste on your shirt instead of on the toothbrush. If you really doubted you could do something, you would at the very least adapt, and probably work to avoid it.

Historically the simplest of actions have had a profound impact on society. Sitting and walking have changed history. In 1960 four men did an everyday thing with confidence - they sat down at a shop to order coffee. That alone was not a difficult action, but it was the specific choice of carrying out that action in that context, because at the time it was anything but routine. These four Black Americans were not welcomed at the 'all White' food counter, but they did not get up when they were asked to leave and their sitting became a powerful action that sparked a series of protest events at that shop that led Woolworths to end its segregation policy. Similarly profound are the actions today of Gretta Thunberg. There is nothing unusual about a teenager sitting or walking, but her conscientious act of sitting outside on a Friday as a 'climate strike' has raised awareness on a global level and drawn support from millions of people across continents. The Chinese proverb of Laozi 'A journey of a thousand miles begins with a single step' is not just a phrase to hang on the wall.

The impact of those first steps rippled out and people noticed. Some changed their attitudes, other were inspired to change their lives. Sometimes with a social cause people join for a particular event, and if not in person they share or retweet a trending hashtag. Trends are not always so profound and are things people look *at*. They watch them as they go past, and may join talking *about* something that is trending, giving a sense of participation and of doing. However, most people simply *don't*. They don't lead. They don't follow. They don't actually do anything at all. Non-action is not simply sitting something out. Through non-doing we actively participate in the opposite of doing, being neither neutral nor passive.

People sometimes think it is an option to just be a bit passive, that they can sit and watch the world pass by like a barge on the waters. From the side lines the structure and flow of society appear to be stable, and even solid. Building on a framework of stability, people enjoy conveniently dining out on a ready-made culture of pre-fabricated items and ideas that can be bought off the shelf and delivered right to us. In this world life is as we expect- people and events run to plan, and that stasis feels reassuring, but in reality everything that lives does change. Every day the world changes and we change physically and mentally. We have agency -a personal choice to do- and can use it to notice and act. But when we attempt to preserve stasis around us, we choose to give up the yes and the can do, effectively putting our agency on the shelf. The decision making capability is still available to us, but sometimes we choose otherwise. Why would we choose not to? Why does the caged bird choose the cage when the door is open? Habit. The cage gives a feeling of safety, and it seems easier to avoid the unknown.

When thinking about the idea of doing, it can be daunting or feel like hard work or just be something we could easily put off until tomorrow. It might even seem silly to think one person living their life, a dot on the map, could possibly change the whole machine with an everyday simple action. Gretta was 15 when she decided to regularly skip school on Fridays and sit in front of the Parliament building, and nobody had heard of her before. She was just a kid, even a kid with Asperger's syndrome, which would certainly have singled her out in previous decades as having special needs, and she would have been dismissed as opposed to being recognized as the material of a world-changing super-star. One year of Fridays on, she was invited to speak to the United Nations, and was subsequently nominated for the Nobel Peace Prize and named Time Magazine's Person of the Year. She is a girl who believed and chose to act. Doing something, no matter how small, has an impact.

It is amazing how the simplest of actions can have an impact, and just like the road, the impact may be one small step at a time, impacting one person, and that is worth while – especially if that one person is you. I asked whose voice we privilege and allow to influence our thinking and decision making. Each of us is important. A voice worth listening to is your own.

The other day I wrote to a friend to comment on an article he had written. Saying what I thought to a friend didn't seem like a big deal at the time and was ordinary for me, but his reply struck me: *Thank you for reading so carefully and taking the time to write back; hardly anybody does that.*

What was he saying? Hardly anybody does what – talk to each other? He was articulating something about wider society: *Most people don't*. That sentence could apply to so many situations and people; and their avoidance is not because they can't. The small action I took – to read something and talk to someone, was not actually challenging in any way, but it did make a difference. Why do people not do things? It is not for lack of capability. We can do so much more than we realize. The action of acknowledging and conversing created connection and in life the affirmation of connection is valued.

When an individual believes in themselves and combines the inclination to act with the conviction to do, this affects change. Repeated actions build on one another and looking at examples across history can illustrate just how possible it is to change the societal fabric around us. Returning to the Chinese proverb about all long journeys starting with one step, it is important to realize that change does not happen instantly. Even before the first action, the element of change is present. It begins with a real mental understanding that you can widen your perspective. A shift in perspective is a change seen externally by nobody, but it is perhaps the most profound step for an individual to take. It enables a view of possibility that can be applied to situations now and in the future. Seeing and awareness become a catalyst for the way we choose and undertake tasks and processes in our lives.

Your own building block

Understanding and mentally acknowledging that we are responsible, on a fundamental and personal level, for our actions gives us agency. By responsible I do not mean simply for the consequences, but the *decisions* we make, whether or not to act, how, when, and with whom. We are responsible for the thinking that goes on between the seed of an idea and the decision to do something. When you recognize and direct your thinking it is like becoming your own Lego brick instead of being one that is already committed to a space on the grid in the instruction's schematic diagram. We are taught conformity and passive participation in many aspects of life, but we can learn to allow the possibility of novelty into the patterns we perceive. When we do this the fabric of our understanding becomes broader, three dimensional, living, and we can become part of it as the weaver instead of the woven. We can invoke agency and choose how we think and what we pursue.

The process of becoming aware of our thinking is about incorporating the pause that inhibits habit into our processes of doing. Like in Alexander Technique, it provides that moment of extra time that enables and allows us to welcome new possibilities. With this time comes our active awareness, where thinking about thinking can begin. This is metacognition. In this setting, metacognitive processes are another unseen part of actions that happen between realising or having an idea or encounter and deciding to act. Metacognition is less explicitly a part of the psychological theory of how people function socially as thinkers in everyday life. In social cognitive theory, there are personal influences which cover aspects of people including their personal perceptions and beliefs, ranging from expectations to fears to ideas of identity and people's situatedness within the environment around them. Metacognition is an active personal process and happens both before and after the decision that yes, you can do something. When thinking how to decide, we think about processes and situations, and reflect (before, while, and after we do something). We consider all we know about the object or situation from various angles and whatever other factors may be related to it.

We think. This is something we can individually own. Nobody can think for you, it is something instigated and directed by you. Having control over such fundamentals as thinking and really knowing that directed thought leads to conscious choice is a big deal, and may be a genuinely new thing to realize. Some people will say – ah, but I choose exactly what I do. Do you? It is surprising how much habit rules us, and when we do take control of a situation, then, like adding one brick on another, you can build your own... *(fill in your own blank here).*

Thinking is personal and can be examined by reducing it to isolated instances. Getting good at enacting our thinking and building the positive momentum to make this into a good habit takes time. Sometimes personal change takes months or years. Many people don't undertake the change of taking control of their actions through deliberate thought and active metacognitive processes because they are waiting for it to happen TO them. This is a side-effect of our pre-packed instant lifestyle. A change that happens to you without your involvement is likely to resemble what happens when people aim for stasis. Standing still is actually a form of regression, atrophy, as the world and life continues to move forward. Looking at an example that applies more widely, a visible positive societal change happens slowly, over generations and involves the momentum of many people realising they can do whatever it is.

People refer to being on their path in life, where they follow from one expected task to the next, creating a seemingly 'natural course of events' which adheres to expectations. Again, this could be great for some, if this path is chosen with awareness. The general population does not practice metacognitive reflection and is in fact pretty nonchalant about following a pre-laid path, and even will ignore walls or obstacles, especially if their basic needs are covered so they them feel warm, protected, and well fed. However, becoming actively aware of and responsible for what you do on a personal level: the thinking, is one of the biggest changes an individual can affect, and is both a change and a choice. The choice of thought is under your own control and happens from within. The key to finding your 'yes' is in being aware, thinking, understanding, allowing, and choosing to believe and listen to your own voice, and then to act on it.

Choosing differently

Today I've woken up to an icy winter morning, and over the past few weeks, in our household we had a great turn-out of things. For us it was the right time to go through the accumulated stuff and pass on to others anything of use or recycle what was not worth using again. After delivering everything to the relevant people or places - charity shops, jumble sales, or the recycling centre, it felt great. Had it not been the right time though, it would not have happened or would have been a devastating process. The idea of *you really should do this because it's good for you* or *we're all doing it – you should do it with us* may be said with good intentions and might be really practical advice. When coerced, actions are not our own and don't have the same positive possibilities. Even when well intentioned, how often have New Year's resolutions quickly become tedious and annoying, and then forgotten? A New Year's resolution to give up smoking or starting a daily exercise routine could also be a really well-intentioned promise, but when done for or because of someone else, it is far less likely to be something you own and feel personally invested in. When decisions come from you, they have a different relevance and gravitas. Doing something because someone told you to do it is not the way to find your yes.

Instead of thinking specifically of achieving change or of doing things or imagining some result in the future, bring it all back to what happens well before any visible action takes place. Remember you have the capacity to think. Thinking fits within the personal realm of how people function psychologically (the main components of human behaviour being the personal – you and all you bring to a situation, the environment around you, and the actions/interactions that take place between you and things / people around you). The internal processes of thought are essential and are critically where we assimilate or compile information to decide on anything. It is where we first assess what we know and make any choices at all: decisions about belief, about desire, about capability, about what we want to do. When you make one of those first, and very important decisions, when you choose to think, know that in thinking you have *choice*.

Recently someone said to me: *I was truly an expert parent until I had kids....* They said how it was so easy to make and dictate assumptions about how things should be, especially for other people's children - what outcome should be expected in a given situation, and expectations of how children should behave, what they should do, and even what path in life they should take.

Sometimes we are bound by expectations that feel imposed by those around us and by society in general, in terms of our role in life and permissible courses of action available to us. Societal norms can be seen to change over time, especially when looking at them from a distance. Take the acceptability of smoking for example. Looking at ads from the 1950s it was seen as glamourous, alluring, and something that people of a certain level of intelligence did. If someone walked into a public space, say a library, now and lit up a cigarette, I doubt they would be looked upon as being a suave intellectual. Looking back, it's easy to be amazed that societal patterns go seemingly unquestioned by many living with them at the time, but consider that when you're in the midst of something you may not even realize there is anything to question. I've watched my children question older generations, asking 'how could they live with that?' (specifically thinking about a lack of freedom or opportunity) and the reply often comes – *life was just like that.* The daily grind can wear people down and it is not uncommon to hear: *I have to do this. I can't change that. My family/friends are relying on me – I don't have a choice.* Even today people don't notice what is around them because they haven't been taught how to look critically, and nobody has given them explicit permission or encouragement to question. Why rock the boat? If we learn to ask, we can notice things around us and be more active in our choosing.

What happens, though, when opportunities are presented without imposed expectations and the associated judgement that goes along with them? That person who said they were sure of all the answers before having children *did* have children. Then they faced actually having to live and think through the various situations they judged with such ease, and realized just how individual each situation is. Simply applying assumptions like pass/fail stamps did not work for each of that person's very different children. Just thinking about education, one child went to school, graduated, and became a banker. Another stopped going to formal school and accessed education online as a teenager, taking a route that didn't exist 15 years ago. Yet another stopped school altogether as a teen and worked with the land. There is no one way, and had external expectations dictated their children's paths, it is possible that each would be far less fulfilled in life.

Assumptions

The activity described earlier in this chapter where people consider different uses for everyday objects is more than a game. When we examine that activity from another perspective its wider relevance to how we view the world becomes clear. Consider the following sentences:

There's a pole in my house. No, it is not a structural support. Yes, it is a dance pole.

What are your thoughts? The first sentence is likely to cause you to say *what?* simply because a pole is not a typical item of household furniture and the sentence may not immediately make sense. It might even seem unfinished. For example, you might ask what the pole is for. The second sentence eliminates one possibility of a structural flaw or building works as a reason for having a pole in the house. The third sentence likely brings to mind several, possibly polarized, thoughts. By now you, the reader, know something about me and my family and you are likely to have some mental representation of me as professor, cellist, having a family, being a critical thinker, and by the nature of this book, someone who wants to make a positive difference in the world. You are also likely to conjure separate mental images both of a house and of what sort of pole this could be. When those images collide, with me being the one talking about the pole in *my* house, what happens? (at this point you are wondering if this hypothetical pole is actually in my house) Is your mind an unbiased blank slate where the physicality of the components is simply put in the same space, or are these images accompanied by judgements carried by prejudice and external associations?

There is in fact a dance pole in between my sitting room and our kitchen, and people who visit first ask if the pole is there for structural reasons, to hold up the house, and then if I'm opening a strip club. I assure you my household does not engage in erotica of any sort. The assumptions are amazing though. After an initial period of curiosity, most people are very keen to have a go swinging round like a child on a climbing frame or attempting to test their strength to lift their body up, like doing a chin-up while holding a vertical, instead of a horizontal, bar. It's like an indoor climbing frame.

Not every object in life will conjure such polar images for its use. This serves as an illustrative example demonstrating how society conditions us to have fixed expectations. When we see something, the answer of its use and value is already known to us, predefined for us. This is X and you do Y with X. Why only Y? There is a whole alphabet of other letters that could fit into that sentence, and that's before we even begin to make more possibilities by arranging the letters into words. Awareness involves inquisition and active thought instead of accepting foregone conclusions. It can be a limitation to put the things in our lives into narrowly defined boxes. It would be a grave mistake indeed to label people, *or ourselves*, with fixed assumptions about their roles or capabilities.

Perspectives

By adding a 'thinking about' stage, we begin to conceive of what is possible. When considering the I can, each of us does this from our own unique perspective. My life is different to your life – the place, the people, the culture – and my perspective, as I think, takes into account and is influenced by *all* the components of my life.

Thinking outside is more than just noticing, more than creatively questioning something's use, our thinking is also informed and influenced by the culture of society around us. The community, city, village, neighbourhood, family you live among all impact your understand of situations or possibilities as presented within your culture and setting.

Consider a different cultural perspective from the past. In the feudal system class was predetermined, and the roles of peasants were firmly defined. Family structures too were set. For example women had a certain role (in the home and to have children), and convention determined the career for even the children of the gentry: the first born owned the land, the second entered military service, the third joined the law, fourth became a priest, and the youngest became a tradesman. Of course these were destinations for the sons; girls were all raised to be married off and produce babies. Fortunately these archaic practices faded in the 17th Century, and there are some accounts of children having some say in their futures. Even today though, very real shadows remain from these and other historical practices.

I was recently driven home from the airport by a taxi driver who told me his story of coming to this country for a better life. He told me back home his mother drove a crane, and I asked how she came to have that job. He explained that even until the early 1980s there was a selection process for who did what in life. If you were in the top 10% of your high school you were selected to go on to university. If you were in the next bracket below, you attended a technical college. The next group down learned a trade, and the others did semi-skilled or manual labour jobs. His mother learned a trade and as a result worked the crane in the construction yard. He wasn't chosen to go to university and so he joined the military. I asked him if he had a choice and he said he never thought about it.

His story was interesting and slightly baffling as it was a story of life from such a different perspective. This career allocation was intended to develop people's most promising qualities, to grow their talents to be productive and valuable for society. What a wonderful opportunity if you are in the right place and that career is what you want to do, or it could be a very unfortunate dictate that puts someone on a completely undesired path for their future. What if you miss out because someone somewhere drew a pre-determined line in the sand, and you didn't have the chance to have the experience or mastery at that moment in time? Does that mean you really can never do that job?

It is a popular misconception that learning must take place at a certain age or it's too late. The idea that if you haven't 'made it' by the age of X then you really won't make it is a fallacy. It is entirely possible that someone has not yet had the opportunity to learn. Accomplishment in any discipline takes time and dedication, and as long as the capability and commitment are there – why can someone not learn? Today life holds many possibilities and the traditional boxes defining who can do what in life are not so rigid as they once were. People do decide to learn at all ages. At the other end of life's spectrum, the concept of retirement has all but evaporated in modern society, as people continue on with four or more careers throughout their lifetime. The taxi driver's story about his mother driving the crane made me think: through what lens do each of us think? *Yes I can* may mean something different to different people. Realising the orientation of the setting in which we are placed is an important step.

Modern society teaches that valuable progression in life has to do with accumulation of things, money, or a job in an office. Is money the goal? For some people it is, and for others defining value by money means nothing. What is your goal? When you say *yes*, what is it you are saying yes to and what comes next?

The game

To understand what is your *yes* we have to look perceptively and understand. Here's a scenario that acts as a metaphor to help enable understanding. Imagine you are playing games in a room full of games and other players. You are playing the Game of Life, and you have been around the board three times, gathered quite a head of steam. Your game is going really well - you are working toward a certain trajectory, with goals and an understanding of how to get there. Looking over to another table to see how someone else is doing, you notice they appear to be to be somehow starting on a totally different level. You don't understand how it's possible that they might not even have considered that they could just go around the board and collect a reward, but they have no intention of doing that. Upon closer inspection, you realize that person is not even on the same game board. In fact, they are playing Go Fish, not the game of Life. Their game has entirely different rules and that seems ok with them, whereas you would not want to play that game at all. Different people are playing all sorts of games, each with their own objectives; some want to win, some are just enjoying the social company, others just like hopping one square to the next.

Is it possible in life that different people are doing the

equivalent of playing a whole range of games? When you see someone else's game, do you look at their game through their eyes, or do you assume they should play the same game as you and wonder if they realize they aren't even on your board yet? But their *yes* might not be on your board at all. Sometimes we attempt to help people by putting them on whatever game we are playing when that may not be where they want to be at all. Progress is not confined to climbing ladders, promotion or following the rules of someone else's game. How then does anyone find out about other games, other possibilities? How do we find out what's out there and what is possible? What game are you playing? Is there an end goal? Should there be a finish line? Are there stages in your game?

Step out in looking.

A friend from Brighton had relatives come to visit. These relatives took the train from their village in Scotland and really had never been out of the country. They came from a place where there were on average 5 people per hectare of land, and there was a shop not too far away. Coming to Brighton was really meeting an alien world beyond any concept of that they didn't know existed outside the movies. Feeling both lost and overwhelmed, they had no idea what to do or how to take it all in, as all the rules for their normal way of being changed or seemingly dissolved.

Some people can and do cope with emersion in completely new settings, but only if they are mentally prepared for change and know how to make quick assessments, judgements, and are willing to adapt as they go along. If a situation is genuinely beyond your conceptual understanding, a natural reaction may be akin to a small child hearing something they do not understand or like: They can't turn off their hearing, so they have to eliminate it some other way. The immediately accessible options are to either go to sleep, which effectively turns off their conscious awareness of hearing, or to make an even louder noise by screaming or crying to drown out the offending sounds, and make it seem to 'go away' from their perceptual picture of now.

Encountering anything new is tricky. When a difference, whether a person, thing, attitude, or idea is met by you, first there is perception (which is no small step- having *noticed* is a huge thing in itself), then comes your internal consideration and assessment. Engaging with this consciously involves metacognition. You could decide to ignore whatever is new, reject it, accept it, even embrace it. Wherever your decision sits on the spectrum, change is involved. Simply because this new something entered your experience, like putting a stone in a stream, there is an element of 'new'. Taking the active decision to allow and see what is around you welcomes change. By deciding to interact with our surroundings, we allow ourselves to experience more fully. This perceptive awareness means a questioning, exploration, and daring to take a few new steps.

Choose differently

I can, but do I choose? Why should I?

It is work to organize thoughts, decisions, and actions, and life constantly moves forward in time. Without change, we progress toward a state of chaotic entropy, and life requires that active engagement. Entropy (decay) is a physical tendency when we sit still, however growth and order are building blocks of the natural living world. Keeping together and focused is a choice and it does take organisation and energy.

Choosing is not a simple yes/no decision, it involves personal, internal processes where you acknowledge and give yourself permission to make that choice. Knowing you are allowed to explore opens a door; it's a ticket to ride. However, one thing that goes along with permission is an acceptance of uncertainty. Every time you take a step, there is an element of uncertainty as to whether your foot will land correctly and support you. It is just possible that you slip or turn your ankle or even just wobble a bit. For each person there will be a balance between the willingness to risk and the allowance of failure. Perhaps we should call it stumbling, as even with walking, when you fall down, it might be technically a momentary 'failure' to walk, but it is very rare that a stumble or tumble stops someone ever walking again. It is important to walk at your own pace, to own your destination, with your own purpose.

Lifting the curtain can be difficult:

> The bird *likes* to sing in its cage.
> The rat has fun in its maze.
> I am lord of my days.

Understanding and mentally visualising choices that cannot be physically seen can be overwhelming. It's a bit like asking someone if they like mandioca, when they have no idea it is a Brazilian root vegetable that can be cooked like chunky potato wedges. It is very difficult to begin to imagine without at least something familiar to act as a reference.

Thinking about life and choices as a game, what does your ideal game look like? Who are the players? Are there cards or pieces? How do you move? Forward, sideways, backwards, or does the board move around you? Do you role the dice and leave it to chance or always move one square at a time? Is it a game that can be won? Are there goals? Do you make the goals or rely on something already written on the game itself?

Are you already playing? Have you ever dared to stop and look up? Or under the board? Or to jump completely off the table and land somewhere else?

Turn the table

That is a long list of questions, and when examining how and what you think, taking a step sideways to consider an analogy with something more familiar can demystify the situation and make it approachable.

Over the years I have always played games – from jigsaw puzzles and board games, to Atari, PC games loaded via cassette, and yes, current platform games too. We enjoy games in our household and one in recent years that caught the imagination of my children is Super Paper Mario. It's a game about a likeable cartoon handyman who progresses through a storyline solving puzzles, finding treasure, and defeating baddies. It's a jovial game with catchy music that keeps you on your toes. The unique and clever thing about this game is it switches, on command of the player, between 2D and 3D gameplay. Progress is not directly stepwise; you do not simply roll the dice and go to the next (obvious) move, but you really do need to think more widely to envision the possibility of what could be and how you could use that to access your goal. By switching from the flat 2D platform 'map' to an interactive 3D world, the whole visible field on screen rotates, allowing the player to 'see' differently. It twists the traditional expectation of gameplay by combining the analogue board game with the simulated three dimensions possible with modern graphics.

Making a habit of looking for possibilities beyond the obvious next step or the next line in the book and beginning to write your own path takes skill and practice. The different perspectives give rise to metacognitive thought, and when we begin analytically thinking, we question and challenge things. What is the dictated value? Are we told what to expect- what *should* be? How does one win? Is the goal money? What if the goal was something else besides gaining some material reward? Or is a goal beyond physicality a sign or symptom of someone who is already privileged to have enough? Are you locked into this game? Are there other players and can the game keep going if you step outside, off the board and move in a completely different direction?

There are some fundamental truths that all people need to

have as basic components in life. Everybody must eat. Everybody must sleep. We age. We breathe. We do need one another. Certainly in my metaphoric game these things are respected and valued. What would be in your game that you value? Are there things that you don't want there?

Answering this swathe of questions may help guide you to what you might build into your game. Importantly, in your game what do you want? I'm not sure that's a single answer question, but more of something that has added facets like a disco ball with lots of little mirrors that make up the overall shimmer. In my game I would like to be healthy and exercise. I would like to focus on being with people and sharing the connection of experience that goes beyond the bounds of words, with others. I want there to be fun and laughter. Start that brainstorm and bring to mind those things that are important to you.

Now after having articulated a few of your ideals, let's turn to a few practical considerations.

As a simple exercise consider what you do with your time. Take a small chunk of the day, one of the bits that is not scheduled by someone else for you (not time while you are at your job, for example) and list what you do. For me I might examine what happens in the morning after I wake up and before I leave the house:

I wake up and lean over the bed to turn off the alarm on my phone. Then, since picking up the phone to turn off the alarm causes the screen to light up, I have a look and click on a couple different icons. My eye might be caught by someone's picture or something someone said on one of two or three different social media sites, and then just in case someone has said something interesting, I keep looking for a bit. Scrolling and scrolling sometimes happens. More days than not I'll pick up my laptop (yes, while I'm still in bed) and check my emails, deleting spam and sifting through whatever arrived overnight. If I'm not careful I can spend a half hour or more *doing exactly nothing but going on autopilot.*

Other people might have a routine that involves a long cup of coffee and sitting, half awake. You might consider your morning time or take another small stretch of day, before, after, or between other activities and question what you do and whether it aligns with what you *want* to do. Is there a way we could use some of that time another way?

Perception and awareness are a start, then we can make choices. When we act on that yes, using our sense of agency, and understand achievement it means we can go forward (or sideways or up or down or whichever way we choose) as we each really begin to play our own game.

CHAPTER THREE
Self-efficacy and the Self

I like to imagine a person's self to be like a disco ball: although it does make a whole, it is not just one glittering ball, but has lots of tiny components – each small individual square of mirror reflects a different aspect of that person's self. The separate parts come together to form how we view ourselves as a whole person. The way we think about ourselves, how we feel valued by different people, the roles we play as parent, child, friend, lover, teacher, boss, customer, - in all the areas of our lives, how we align ourselves by what we value and like, there are so many different aspects to what makes up a whole person that it is not simple to fully define the idea of 'self'.

On this shimmering disco ball of the self, our self-efficacy beliefs make up individual mirror tiles. They are not the whole view of the self, or something that defines our identity. They are individual, personal beliefs about each of the things we do. They are really specific, for example, *I believe I can ride a bike,* as opposed to the general idea of: *I am good at sport.* Or you could hold the self-efficacy belief that: *I am sure I can cook that dessert to perfection,* but a more broad statement like: *I'm a chef* describes part of your identity and not your self-efficacy beliefs. Self-efficacy beliefs make up a slice of the many thoughts, ideas, and beliefs that combine to form a person's 'self'. The more general views we hold about ourselves, our self-concept or self-image cover wider aspects of the self and take into account social situations and comparisons. In contrast, self-efficacy beliefs are not based on external comparisons, but they are solely a consideration of how we believe in our own capabilities to do things.

Sources of self-efficacy

In psychology Albert Bandura was a founder of social cognitive theory, which explains how people function in everyday life and includes our environment, our behaviours and what we do, and our own personal thoughts and attitudes. It was Bandura who first introduced self-efficacy in the late 1970s. In his original experimental studies, he identified four main influences on our self-efficacy beliefs and and listed them as a taxonomy going from the most influential: our experiences of doing things, to observations, to social interactions and advice from others, to the awareness of our bodies and physical signs (e.g. sweaty hands, a nervous tummy, strong muscles), which is the least of the influences.

It makes sense that once we have done something and mastered it, there are grounds to believe in our being capable of doing a similar task if it was presented to us in the future. Our actual achievements (and failures), whatever we *do*, act as the strongest influence on our self-efficacy beliefs, creating a foundation for our can-do confidence. However, not everyone has done everything, and before you do something for the first time you will still hold beliefs about how well you can do whatever it is. Bandura listed observational experience as the next strongest influence on self-efficacy beliefs. Watching someone else 'perform' a task can be inspiring and influential and can be a strong influence on our own beliefs even if you haven't done it yourself.

There can be different sorts of observing. Not everything has to be seeing the professionals glamorously performing on the big screen. Watching someone who is still learning and not necessarily a master but is coping with difficulty and working towards achieving a goal can also have a real impact on us. Take a cooking show for example, where there may be people preparing a dish and the audience has a window into the entire process. We get to observe the *how*. Watching someone else go through pitfalls and figure a way out can give us a sense that the task is possible, as we have seen someone else achieve it. By watching people learn we can better understand the skills needed to get from the start to the finish. Depending on the task, this observational process can be even more believable and meaningful when the person being observed is somehow similar to you. They may have similar experience, or come from the same background, or have a similar attitude or goal, or be physically the same size or shape as you – there will be something about them and the way they do whatever it is that makes you believe *you* could fill those shoes and succeed in that task too. For example watching competitive gymnastics might kindle in a teenager's self-efficacy beliefs for doing gymnastics whereas it may not inspire the same self-beliefs in that teenager's grandparents, simply because they may view themselves as different to the very young and flexible performer.

To a lesser extent, self-efficacy beliefs are influenced through social persuasion in the conversations and interactions we have with others; people can encourage or dissuade us. However, if someone is simply told that they can achieve a task, they may still never attempt it. There could be all sorts of reasons why, and the overall influence can be minimal. However, someone might say just the right thing at the right time, and that can make all the difference to someone's confidence in their capabilities to do something. The least influential of Bandura's influences are the physiological signals that happen when we think about and approach tasks. Before I speak to a group I might get cold hands or a dry mouth as a sign of nerves, but these physical signs are not going to override the influence of my past experience. I'm likely to ignore them and speak with confidence anyway. Similarly, tiredness or stress may also affect someone's belief in how capable they are to do something, and may impact the quality of delivery, but it is unlikely to stop them.

The influence of self-efficacy

Self-efficacy beliefs are specific to each thing we do. You may have really strong self-efficacy for one thing and rock-bottom beliefs in your capabilities to do something else. Because they apply so specifically, it would be possible to think that the impact is also narrow and might not really have much impact on our whole selves, but in fact our self-efficacy beliefs have a huge and broad influence. It is rather like our self-efficacy beliefs are a fine thread that is woven through everything we do and therefore a golden thread can make the overall fabric of our lives something quite regal. Self-efficacy beliefs influence the pursuits we choose to undertake and how we approach them. As we engage with the various processes as we prepare and learn, each of those choices becomes another action in the catalogue of our accomplishments. Realising this can open a door to transferability that can permeate far beyond any specific task.

Self-efficacy beliefs influence goal setting and analytic thinking. People with higher self-efficacy tend to choose more challenging tasks and persist longer rather than giving up at the first sign of difficulty. They are more resilient, do not shy away from the possibility of failure, and as a result they use more strategic approaches to ensure they complete what they start. People with strong self-efficacy beliefs also attain better results in the end. These beliefs are central to everyday functioning and, whether we are consciously aware of them or not, they are held about every task we undertake.

Bandura made a landmark contribution to psychology by introducing the concept of self-efficacy and its key influences. Dozens of researchers have since examined self-efficacy through formal experiments with controlled settings to show how these beliefs influence achievement, how they are indeed specific to tasks, and to highlight their existence across all sorts of contexts from music to sport to business to education to teaching to parenting to health care to recovering from trauma, and the list goes on. In short, research has demonstrated these beliefs are important to life. What is missing from the formal experiments and literature is the explanation of *how* people get from encountering some influence to actually believing for themselves.

The study of self-efficacy

Research and questionnaires

In psychology study happens via experiments, and the most popular way to gain insight into people's self-efficacy beliefs has been through questionnaires. Researchers have designed questionnaires ranging from a single question (which doesn't really cut it when looking at these complex beliefs) to questionnaires comprising whole batteries of questions designed to capture elements of the different facets of someone's self-efficacy beliefs. The approach is praiseworthy, but whole idea of having self-efficacy questionnaires is artificial. It captures one side. It is rather like trying to define friendship on paper. That's super-hard and there will be so many differences. The approach to researching self-efficacy goes something like this: People are invited to take part in a research study, and historically with self-efficacy research this tends to involve completing a questionnaire. Ideally the questionnaire is completed as close to actually doing whatever the task is as possible, in an attempt to somehow get an accurate to-the-moment picture of someone's self-efficacy beliefs. This approach is not all bad; I've designed questionnaires myself and used them with hundreds of people in academic studies.

In reality though, the moment you complete a questionnaire, ticking boxes or using a percentage to rate *how confident you are that you can…* is not really either the moment or representative of the mental method used to make that gut decision of *I can*. It is not usually done on a conscious level. There is something inherently artificial, or at least one step removed from the truth about attempting to putting that process down on paper. In practice people don't usually understand or know how they function in the same way you could 'show your working' for a complex algebraic equation. Yes, the idea of making a self-efficacy judgement might be brought to the forefront, deliberated, and negotiated in various settings, and a questionnaire could highlight this, but the decision of when and how much you believe in your capabilities is something arrived at from deep within, in a flash – it happens even between the blinks of the eye. A questionnaire asks people to consciously re-enact and analyse a process that few are aware even happens. Quantifying a feeling in the form of words and tick boxes is an artificial representation, and at best comes close to the truth.

"To turn experience into speech – that is, to classify, to conceptualize, to grammarize, to syntactify it- is always a betrayal of experience, a falsification of it; but only so betrayed can it be dealt with at all, and only in so dealing with it did I ever feel a man alive and kicking." - *End of the Road*, by John Barth

In terms of studying these beliefs from an educational and research perspective, it makes perfect sense to use questionnaires, since language is one of the few ways we can gain insight into what others are thinking without using some invasive method like a neurological scanner. Even if questionnaires are the next best thing to actually knowing what someone thinks, they are still like studying a shadow is to knowing the real thing: second best. If we each filled out a questionnaire we could very possibly get an approximation of our beliefs, and depending on the thoroughness of the questionnaire, maybe a very good approximation, but it is an artificial exercise to verbally articulate something that is not inherently created in words, and certainly not in terms of a questionnaire-style rating scale.

Observation & noticing

It is far easier to notice thinking when we are the onlooker and not the one doing the thinking. Sometimes when we watch a person do something, we can pinpoint the moment they make a decision and then watch the actions that follow. With the wisdom of having seen it happen, we can make the person aware of the processes that have just unfolded. To make someone aware we could straight-up talk them through and say: *'Hey, did you realize you did this? I could almost see you thinking.'* That may sound beyond weird, but this happens often with parents and small children even with the most simple things.

When you reached to take that slice of pizza from the dish, I could see you thought it looked good, but did you stop and think it was hot before you burned your mouth with that first bite?

The analysis of whether the pizza was ok to eat sounds really simple and like one of those things someone should know instead of something you might have self-efficacy beliefs about, but every action we take has an underlying sense of judgement about our capabilities for doing it. If there is a task and I am confident I can do it, part of that confidence involves understanding what is required to carry out the task. In the case of the person taking the pizza slice, understanding that they could hold it is part of the task and then knowing it was cool enough to eat, or how to cool it down, is another part. It is possible to have a false sense of self-efficacy when the task is not thought through or understood. When we decide and approach other tasks in our lives, the process is not all that different (if sometimes less tasty).

Getting anyone to be aware of their beliefs and think through the minutia of their decisions and ensuing actions involves mentally going through everything, all the processes, skills, physicality, external factors, people, things, all the different components and understanding how they work and what demands are placed on you. This is easier to imagine from the point of view of an observer who has just seen something and explains; it is as if the explainer replays elements of the situation in slow-motion, explaining and analysing all the processes that have taken place. This is something we can do for ourselves, but it is easier to initially understand from an external perspective.

This act of becoming consciously aware of what were assumed to be automatic subconscious judgements, self-efficacy beliefs, about what we set out to do, and learning how these beliefs influence our actions can give us the tools to notice and then change how we think and believe. It takes work, and practice – repetition - to learn and reinforce the skill of being aware. Then it takes even further awareness to step inside our thought process and control aspects of what we once assumed to be automatic reactions or perhaps didn't notice happening at all. Becoming aware enables you to react in the moment, take a new planned path, and actively re-constitute your belief forming process.

Most people do what they do because it is what they have always done or known and there has never been a particular reason to think or do otherwise. Consider your own learning: Whatever you learned in school, you probably did and still do in the way your teacher told you. Many times that will also reflect how your teacher was taught… they do what they were told and have passed it on. Without considerable forethought and awareness of the specific needs of individual students, people (in formal education, at home, and in work environments) often teach however they were taught, regardless of whether it is effective or not.

Breaking this pattern of unthinking-doing takes considerable re-learning, as habits can be longstanding and deeply rooted. It is possible to become aware of our processes and take an active control of them, however, this takes effort. Importantly, we must remember change is possible.

Take the Alexander Technique as a practical example. Matthias Alexander studied himself and figured out not only that he had physical tension problems and his problem was a very common problem, to a lesser degree of severity, in the general population, but he also figured out how he could correct these problems for himself and others. He learned to get inside his thoughts and influence his decision making. First he noticed by observing that when humans get scared, for example by a loud noise, they react by tensing up. People tighten up around their neck and shoulders. They also adopt this neck tightening in all sorts of other situations beside a boom or shocking surprise. Minor surprises, mental surprises or worries can all induce the same physical reaction. Alexander noticed he was doing this when on stage – the audience was his threatening equivalent of a loud noise, and although he was not aware of consciously choosing to tense up, this was not a reflex, and he learned to actively notice and stop creating this tension.

We can examine a specific example of retraining responses from how Alexander Technique reteaches someone how to go from sitting on a chair to standing up. Standing up is not threatening, but habitually in preparation for getting up from a chair, people will lean forward and tilt their head back to level their gaze. This shortens the muscles in the back of the neck, causes tension in both the neck and shoulders, and also breaks the natural neutrality of the spine, and then with this induced accumulation of tension they stand up. That head motion and the chain reaction it causes *seem* to be automatic, like a reflex, and definitely seem subconscious, but we are simply unaware of it, and we can learn to change our pattern of behaviour. It is a very deeply learned and engrained habit that we have reinforced over thousands of repetitions of sitting and standing. The entire premise for the Alexander Technique is to retrain and undo negative underlying physical habits that create tension, like throwing your head back and inducing undue tension when standing up.

Alexander teaches the person to first *stop*. The act of stopping and recognising what you are doing instead of simply allowing the habit to continue, in fact begins to undo what would otherwise masquerade as an automatic response. The next step in this technique is to introduce a new and positive process by consciously giving yourself a command similar to: 'The head moves forward and up so the neck can soften and lengthen.' This sort of mantra encourages the natural neutral spinal position to be actively retained instead of squashing the space at the base of the neck by throwing back the head. What once seemed to be 'just the way it is' - an unconscious chain reaction, is interrupted, paused, and a new pattern of behaviour is introduced.

This process can be taught in other settings, for both mental and physical tasks, by methodically slowing down whatever the process is, noticing it, and training people to go through the steps they would like to take. As perception and awareness grow, each positive experience can reinforce a new pathway for decision making. If this way of thinking is to become a new normal, it has to be reinforced, and reinforced some more, as we begin to rewrite the cumulative experience of habit.

Anchoring and practical situations

Using people and things around us can serve as external markers to stretch or give a context to our understanding of what we can do. This brings a new level to observational experiences, and they can have an added impact if used as an anchor, to frame or guide your progress. The important thing when using this sort of external information is that we are using the anchor as a marker to frame our own capabilities in terms of us and not in relation to them. This is not a judgement of social comparison, but an active tool to develop ourselves, as in: *I've done this, but I could do that*, instead of using social comparisons to be a limiting definition of what is possible for us: *They did that so I must not be able to do that.*

I used the concept of anchoring in my high school PE class. Everyone took part in track and field training, and we ran in groups so the track was not overcrowded. I actively choose to run against the people I knew would always beat me, but that was not a problem for me. I didn't do it to fail every time, instead it was more like saying I wanted to play with the A-team, and I wanted the chance to rise to a challenge. This was one way I could push myself.

These fast runners were a living manifestation of what I wanted to be able to do. Their speed was a goal beyond what I had done, or could readily conceive of doing by myself at that moment. Using them as an externalisation of my goal, allowed them to act as an anchor for me. It didn't matter that I could not imagine myself running a 7 minute mile, because I could physically stand next to someone who not only could, but did. This meant I could push myself harder than if I was running alone because I ran against some speedy individual instead of against whatever limits I thought I had. If I ran against myself, I would have the feeling of my own muscles and the empty space around me to judge how I was doing, and without someone else or a giant time-clock, it was certainly easier to rest in the comfort of whatever I felt instead of accessing the untapped possibilities of my capability. I almost always came last in those track races, but I never thought of it as losing *to someone else*, because it had nothing to do with the other person or my rank at the end of that heat. Every time I knocked a few tenths of a second from my previous time I felt like I won. I was pushing to compete with myself and the external anchor had to do with me stretching and developing my own self-efficacy beliefs.

Before using an anchor successfully you have to first acknowledge the fact that you can; that door to belief has to be opened. Then you can push or do or choose how or what comes next. The difference between capability and ability is simple on paper: ability is about being already able- a measurement of a current state, how much you can deliver at this moment, whereas capability is undefined, and not about where you are now but about the possibility of maybe someday. Working with capability means entering a constant state of learning, which includes both elements of failure and growth, and definitely involves organized, dedicated effort.

The processes of growth, on a basic level, involve the creation of something new. Birth is something that we all experience at the start of our lives, physically we grow until a certain point in life, sometime in our early 20s. With that in mind if we look back at the phrase 'grown-up', discussed in Chapter 1, we may now come up with different answers to what that means. There is a point at which the body stops growing taller or creating new bone, and in that sense part of us is *done* with the physical aspect of growing. However, growth as a process continues to happen until we die. Every day we grow new blood cells, produce the inside juices to digest and convert food into useful energy to live and rebuild our bodies. Our bodies require growth just to maintain the stasis of everyday life. Somehow though, people stop entertaining the idea that mentally and even physically into old age we can continue to grow and develop strength, skills, and competencies. People think they know things, and once a fact or skill is learned, that is enough, but there is always decay. The natural path of people is to go away from, both physically and mentally: without deliberate thought and action there is decay. It takes attention and work just to maintain stasis. When we stop growing, the repertoire of what is within our current ability decays. Muscles atrophy, we forget, and our brains and bodies turn into something metaphorically like three day old pasta.

Growth is possible

Whether we have the confidence to do or firmly maintain the idea that we really don't think we can do certain things, our self-efficacy beliefs are typically something we do feel on a gut level. This does not mean they are built into us and cannot be changed. Many seemingly unconscious judgements about self-efficacy that we make are more akin to learned habits, that are actually changeable, as opposed to hard-wired reflexes. For example the fact that my leg goes boing when a doctor hits my knee with a rubber mallet is different to the fact that I tend to duck when a ball is thrown to me whereas my son catches it. My choice of duck instead of attempt to catch is the result of my self-efficacy beliefs about my capabilities to catch the ball. I spent years in school sitting on the bench not playing ball whereas my son had a decade of playing cricket in school.

As with any situation, state of being, whether in our heads or a practical situation, we can do something about it. We can rearrange, realign, reorder, catalogue, change, and create new. Change is by no means a quick or easy process. From the everyday stuff of dishes (like dealing with that three day old pasta) or laundry to taking on a new hobby, or the more abstract thinking involved in changing an old habit, growing can definitely feel uncomfortable as we shift and change from one way to another. We can feel the physical strain of change and the fatigue of exercising and this is true when we exercise our mental capacities too. Whatever growth entails, through active awareness and deliberate and directed thinking we can inform and facilitate growth.

Noticing and realising is the first step. What stage are you at in whatever process you are doing? What's your outlook in terms of how you think about your own capabilities? The things you notice could be that you do indeed think, know, *believe* you can do certain things. Those are important to notice. There will also be things you are not so sure of. It could be you haven't yet figured out how to do something, or you thought you knew how to do it, but like Alexander and his tension, perhaps we realise we're getting in our way and blocking the outcome from happening. The catalyst or reason behind making a change is often to allow for a desired outcome to happen.

When talking about our self-beliefs in how and what we can do, when we understand what's involved with our mental mechanisms and processes and how our internal and external worlds interact, we can be in a position to examine, assess, and make accurate judgements about both where we are now and what we need to do to get to where we're going. However, as with Alexander if we wait until there's a real problem and we've hit a wall, it is pretty late in the day. Change is possible at any time, but it involves work. To *do* the change we can't simply fix it. If my clock reads the wrong time, I can't simply re-position the hands on the clock face to read the correct time – well, I could but it would only appear correct for a moment. A real solution requires me to identify processes and understand how all the underlying mechanisms work. How do the cogs fit together and turn? What impact does one have on the other? Then I can be in a position to notice small things and begin to make adjustments to affect change. We can wait until there's a problem and backtrack to fix it, or we can be motivated to stop, notice, and grow right from the beginning.

To play music, and to be able to play pieces to others, in a concert or public setting, there has to be practice. People don't just pick up an instrument and play it to a wonderful standard on the stage. On my cello, I spend hours and hours working analytically. Music practice is not simply playing through in the same way as you might read a book or watch a film, going from beginning to end, maybe eating popcorn as you go, and then after one go that's enough. With a film or a book the reader or watcher is the audience, a passive recipient, but when playing an instrument the player has to create the content, and that takes actively engaged thought.

For example when I learn a piece on the cello I spend hours mining into the detail to train my thought processes, decision making, and execution so that in performance my physical actions and mental representation of the music can be consistent and reliable. There are coordination issues between the fingers on the hand that holds down the notes on the strings, and then more coordination to get the right hand to pull the bow just at the right time to sound clearly for each fingered note. The sound, the style, the phrasing, the dynamics, the expression, there are so many levels of detail and without continual attention I could lose it in performance, and the music will not quite come out right due to any one of a number of factors. That would mean the listener wouldn't be able to enjoy it.

Even if I could have 100% retention of mental and physical skills, which is not possible because as a human both my mind and my muscles go to mush without training, I still couldn't *do* it without constant attention and awareness. (*That*, right there is me articulating a self-efficacy belief. I am not confident that I can perform music to a standard that I am happy with without a good mental presence. I've made that judgement with an awareness of the skills required for the task and with an understanding of my own abilities, and capabilities to deliver and cope with various challenges that task may present.) Part of that deliberate retraining is knowing that I have attended to the details from various directions and knowing the skills are solid. Through repetition and thoughtful awareness I have reinforced and mastered the different aspects of the music so I know that I can deliver it effectively in a performance. I *know* that I can achieve it. My self-efficacy beliefs are strong and *I believe I can*.

In music, the performance setting is the practical test where these beliefs are demonstrated and confirmed. Music concerts are fairly predictable settings. Whether at a pop or a classical concert, the performer is set apart from the audience, usually on a stage, in a relatively controlled setting and audience is there to witness and experience the musical display and artistry. The performer knows this and prepares accordingly. Just as with the Alexander Technique where a person retrains their thoughts to free their physical response instead of allowing the negative habits to come out, a musician also trains the actions they will carry out during the performance and their anticipated reactions to external factors. Very little external input is allowed into the artist's field of awareness during the performance. Neither a person unwrapping a sweet in the front row to stop coughing or someone coming in late through the door will divert the attention of the performer. Partly this demonstrates a high level of how one can train thinking to be different in preparation for a certain setting, but also this example is not exactly practical in terms of our everyday lives. This sort of performance of skills is both literally and metaphorically staged.

This staging and having an almost experimentally controlled setting happens in athletics as well. Competing as an athlete in the Olympics is certainly not the type of everyday-life setting people find themselves in to test physical skills. It is as if the Olympics is a hugely popular, very formal experiment to observe and assess skill at the highest level. That very specific performance situation has been engineered carefully to strip away any variables that could interfere with the skills demonstration in the sporting events. The external influences are minimized so whatever non-competition components that are left come from a predictable, pre-known set of possible distractions. For example, it is expected that people in the crowd will cheer, the wind will blow, there will be lights on the competitors, and athletes are aware of how many other competitors will be in their event and of exactly what procedures will take place as the games unfold. There are strict guidelines for audience behaviour and stewards are watching to make sure that nothing unexpected happens. Nobody is going to come onto the track and stand in the path of a runner. The Olympics is a controlled environment not unlike an experiment that could be devised in a science lab. It is an excellent setting to observe people who train themselves to have both the skill and belief to deliver in their specific event. There is no doubt that they have very high self-efficacy beliefs, and it is also clear that an elite athlete's vision of their capabilities is well beyond the everyday. These people have anchors in the clouds.

These performance settings are admittedly possibly outside most people's normal experiences, however I do think they serve as accessible examples of how someone can retrain thinking and demonstrate the impact of their efforts. It is highly likely that you have been to a concert or sporting event in person at some point in your life, and most people will have seen a snippet of someone winning an event at the Olympics or of some celebrity performing on stage. (If you have not seen either of these, now is the time to get searching on the internet.) The point is that even if you don't do these things yourself, you can access them as an observer, and hopefully can begin to see elements of the processes described here in action.

When we learn to do something, whether sport, music, cooking, business, or walking to the corner shop, our awareness needs to be equally about training the processes as it is about the experiences. If we are just aware of doing the thing deliberately, but not consciously or actively in control of the processes, then we are unlikely to own them and even if we achieve a goal it is unlikely to *mean* something for us and for our self-efficacy beliefs. When awareness is linked up, it can impact the task at hand and more widely how people approach decisions in life, including seemingly intuitive decisions.

It makes sense that when skills are learned with awareness, a sense of connected, deep learning, and actual belief throughout the learning process, they are more likely to become the new, chosen habit. This positively engrained action can then become a part of our new normal. Beside the skill of learning to enact and own our thought processes, perpetuating this also involves maintaining a certain outlook on reality. Chapter 1 discusses an openness to perceptive detail. In becoming aware, we need to look in an optimistic way. If we are actively aware and looking for new things, we are more likely to find something. It doesn't have to be a specific goal or expectation, but an honest to goodness view of hope for yes - otherwise people would submit to a world of seeming stasis that simply allowed them to slowly retreat into sleep. It is effort to choose the yes, the I can, but to me there really is not another choice.

Impact on our lives

When influence happens

Bandura identified the main types of influence on self-efficacy beliefs, but the way these have an impact in real life does not necessarily fit neatly into a numbered list. It is clear in his experiments where controlled conditions allow for a specific influence to be isolated and studied in relation to a named task, but it is seldom either so neatly presented or simply defined in our lives.

For example when doing something, even the positive experience of mastering a task is not enough on its own to guarantee an important influence on our beliefs. Everyday we do things, accomplish things that we don't really realize or acknowledge as achievements. In order for something to become an influence, the person has to notice, perceive, and be receptive to it. One person's achievement can be thought of as a run of the mill non-event to someone else if they are just going through the motions. This can also happen if they think their accomplishment wasn't actually due to their own skill but because of someone else. For example someone could realistically think: *I have no idea what I'm doing. I was just doing what you told me to do.* In this case there is likely to be little meaning in that action. When we fail to notice the things we do, potential influences on our self-efficacy also go unnoticed, and lie dormant. This lack of noticing the achievement or impact of performance, does however open the door for what would be, according to Bandura's hierarchy, a lesser influence to come forward and actually have a greater impact on our self-efficacy beliefs.

Influence of influences

A story. I went out with my family the other night to catch the sunset as it was the first clear day after a rainy week, and we noticed a flock of birds on the water. I commented, *'Ah look at the Brent Geese,'* and my son said, *'No, those are ducks.'* I said, *'Geese.'* He said, *'but they are ducks.'* We kept walking and I thought I'd take a video on my phone, attempting to capture the quiet, and instead got a second of wind noise followed by a young voice saying, *'but they are ducks…'*! The sunset was lovely, though.

Then the next morning my son and I were walking along the same stretch of seaside and happened to pass the very wise and well spoken neighbor of ours, Brigadier Bill Woodburn. I asked (innocently), 'Bill, those birds, are they geese or ducks?' (I knew very well what they were) and he replied aptly saying, *'Those are Brent Geese and you really should know that by now. I could tell you more about them but you had better be getting on….'* My son gave a little skip in his step and smiled, saying, *'geese?!'* You could almost hear him thinking – well I never knew! The Brigadier called after us saying, *'They are the size of ducks but are definitely geese. They do look a bit like ducks though…'*

So that was it; my son believed him, but he was not willing to believe me the day before. How many times are we told something and we don't believe it until somehow we hear it from someone else? Likewise, how many times do we *do* something and we don't believe we've really done it? For something to be an effective influence on our beliefs, to give us that skip in our step and make us smile, we have to actively listen and believe it.

As a teacher, I've seen many people *do* things, like achieve a good grade in a class that means nothing. I've done it myself many times as a student and in life, going from start to finish because I had to and not taking anything in or paying attention to process or content. There are both high school and university classes where I remember nothing of what I apparently learned, even though I got a good grade for it. I wasn't doing it for me and neither completing the class nor the grades were significant to me or my self-beliefs.

What if traditional mastery of a task does means nothing to us? This could be for various reasons from not noticing to a learned deprivation of value. For example someone who is a cleaner or janitor might devalue their skill because of the (incorrect) external view imposed on them that their job is somehow less important because it is not glamorous, or a woman or ethnic minority may accept the societal view of hearing that their accomplishment is less than the white man who also does the same, or they may have this reinforced not verbally but by being paid less for the same work. Whether the personal disregard for accomplishment comes from a historical pattern of negativity from society, self-talk, or simply not looking at the tasks you do as real accomplishments these negative views mean those achievements are not going to be the amazingly influential boost they might be for someone else. When mastery isn't noticed and doesn't fill the role of the main influence on our self-efficacy beliefs, the other seemingly insignificant influences can be quite powerful.

To override any established self-efficacy beliefs, an influence needs to be recognized as valid by you. Importantly, all the aspects of it need to be genuine. If it is an interaction with someone else, they are likely to be respected and trusted and the situation cannot not be perceived as contrived or manipulative or it will just not work. Another ingredient for these situations is that we are ready to see what is in front of us. Let me demonstrate a situation where noticing can be fertile ground where an experience can influence thinking.

Imagine you are standing at the edge of a lake and on the surface of the water there is stillness. The situation is neutral, but not passive; you are aware and engaged in being present there. You see the water, feel the subtle breeze and sun, and hear the sounds around you. When the stillness is broken by a little 'blurp!' as a fish breaks through from underneath the water to eat an insect, you notice. You probably also acknowledge that noticing by either thinking or saying, *Hey! I saw a fish!*

This noticing and being affected by something can happen in other situations in our lives, where aspects of the setting are neutral. By neutral I mean the obvious pressures associated with a task have been somehow removed. This could be because the situation is different than normal for you, either a new setting completely or where you are not the one delivering the task but observing it. For example, in the story about the geese above, I created a neutral situation where my son was an observer and could watch the respected Brigadier tell me that the birds are obviously geese. This observational experience was genuinely more influential than the direct experience of being told the answer. There was no threat or risk to him as an observer, instead I took the active role of the one being corrected when I was told in no uncertain terms that they were geese. It was a safe situation for him, and when there is not an obvious risk to you then something somebody says, or something you see, or noticing the way you feel in that situation can have a very real impact.

Influence on skills

It is easy to understand if we consciously take responsibility for what we do, we are more likely to look at our thoughts, actions, and accomplishments as being valid and genuinely ours. Each act of mastery, as Bandura called it, adds meaningfully to our portfolio of skills and experiences and this enables us to develop a sense of possibility and growth that goes substantially beyond simply having a mindset because it is backed up by achievement.

What if the impact of an influence is not so straightforward as to realize *I did this* and therefore *I can do that*? What if the influence goes beyond relating to a single task but instead changes your views about a skill or process that is at the root of several, possibly quite separate things you do? There is no reason one of Bandura's named influences cannot affect the understanding of your core capabilities for skills or processes. Identifying a skill or fundamental thought process is somewhat of an abstraction and is less directly visible simply because we usually deliver a skill through tasks and we can see the outputs rather than directly seeing the processes.

Surprising realisations and impact can occur when you find yourself in situations that encourage awareness and have elements of neutrality. These tend to lie outside the normal contextual framework of a task. Once I found myself concentrating intensely on my cello, observing and engaging in deep, critical reflection of all my musical practices. I continued working this way for several months, and in the middle of the process I travelled abroad, and as a visitor in a town I sat having conversations over breakfast with extraordinary people who happened to be leaders in their academic research fields. This setting was far removed from my everyday existence and the associated (or assumed) boundaries and restrictions of my usual settings appeared suspended in this new setting. The 'undefinedness' of it gave the situation a flavour of neutrality.

The months of self-reflective music practice had put me in a heightened frame of awareness and even though these morning conversations over fruit and cake were not planned or about anything in specific, they had an impact for me. The simple fact that there *was* conversation was a form of validation and had a great impact on my self-beliefs about *thinking*. I wasn't performing a specific task, but I was engaging and thinking with respected people who treated me as peers. There was no actual task with an outcome, no appraisal or goal. There was no on the spot analysis, only the encounter itself. The actual task of chatting over breakfast is something common, and not in itself unique. A key to why this situation worked was its genuine neutrality: I neither judged nor felt judged. The experience stayed with me because those who spoke with me were respected, and this made it authentic and valid to me. Without requirement, prerequisite, or prejudice, my thoughts were accepted. This external validation, even though it was not on a formally delivered 'task', enabled a different kind of belief (as I already knew my *capabilities* were there). It planted the seeds of influence for me to make measurable changes in my future actions beyond knowing I *can*. Having an influence that triggered my genuine self-efficacy beliefs opened the door for agency.

Step by step.

The active awareness of our beliefs and of the things around us makes us more receptive to process. It is not a guarantee that we will be looking into the crystal waters of the Caribbean and witness the interaction of our processes and beliefs like fish swimming around the coral reefs. Mentally we will still be swept up in the currents and debris of life and living no matter how much intellectual understanding we hold. Step one is to consider your thinking and awareness of how self-efficacy influences tasks or skills. Sometimes this will be easy to see and hit you like turning on a light, where suddenly you *do* know you can do something and can pinpoint the moment that made you believe, whereas other times the realisation may be more of a slow drip that takes time to soak in, and yet other times it will be months later when you can finally say, 'ah yes that was what happened'. People are unique and *your* perspective cannot be simply duplicated and explained away with a simple x +y = z formula. The impact of an influence on your self-efficacy beliefs is something you will have to notice, reflect on, and recognize for and within yourself.

Once there is an awareness of what is influencing your beliefs and what those self-efficacy beliefs are for, then transferability can be achieved. If you have developed self-efficacy beliefs that are directly related to a single task, a specific performance, then it makes sense that if that task is encountered again, those beliefs can be carried forward to transfer and inform self-efficacy beliefs about the next situation. This is quite limiting though, and it doesn't make sense that an influence is so selectively siloed. These beliefs can transfer across various tasks that also use the same core skills. Think about this as an example:

When learning new words, for example in school when you first learned a word like 'atmosphere', you learned to write it, say it, define it, and importantly **to use it.** In other areas of our lives, sometimes we 'do the thing' but do not reflect holistically on what is involved, the use, the possibilities, or how these can be taken forward in the future. If you have ever learned to sing or play an instrument you may be able to relate. If you played your newly learned piece to someone and then they asked you to play another song, a common reply is, 'Sorry, I don't know anything else, I've only learned this song so far.' The beginner musician rarely looks at the component parts of what they have learned and the possibility of rearranging them into a musical conversation, just like a small child does all the time with thier limited verbal vocabulary. How ridiculous would it be if we only learned words in a single context and had to relearn everything for each story, poem, letter we read or wrote?

Any influence will *initially* impact a specific task being delivered at a specific time in a specific place, and from this starting point relevance and possibly transference can take place. When you reflect and become aware of the component skills involved in whatever you have done successfully, it is possible to realize how skills can be transferred to other settings or situations. Active thinking and reflection allow the impact of a positive accomplishment to go further than being limited to that one situation.

It is unrealistic to think there could be a single, all-encompassing model to predict the subtle impact any influence could have on someone's self-efficacy beliefs and their actions, simply because we are all unique individuals. There may be similar patterns for outcomes, but there will be variation. However, there are some key ingredients integral to allowing and recognising an influence. These have to do with openness, receptivity, removal of assumed barriers and absence of immediate judgement and they lead to the possibility of moving forward through action, as you enact agency.

Recognising and allowing gives rise to allowance for genuine possibility through agency.

CHAPTER FOUR
Motivation

It is a reality that we live in an unequal world where some people have an easier time due to money, geography, or their past experience and opportunities. Examples of strategies and methods for creating an infrastructure for real, sustainable growth are presented in light of perceived and real barriers to achievement.

Growth

Sprouting

Each of my children, somewhere between the ages of 5-7, came home from school gingerly carrying a section of egg carton filled with earth. They had planted a seed and the project was to watch it grow. It was fool-proof. We added a few drops of water each day and sure enough tiny shoots came out of the soil. Amazing. If you stuck me in a cardboard box and gave me a bit of water I'm not sure you would achieve the same up-stretching, fruitful results, but that seed went for it.

The sheer tenacity of plants is baffling. Once the basic conditions are met, they do grow. There is a hunger for growth, and wherever some plants find themselves, they manage to grow whether in the cracks of the pavement or in the knot hole of a tree where a little soil has formed from decayed leaves. The most unlikely places can host growth and plants somehow aren't quite like people in needing to have the right floor plan before they settle.

There are qualities of determination and resilience that can be learned from plants. People's motivation to grow is more complex and not simply fed by external conditions or a stimulus, but can be personally guided and driven by our sense of vision and goal.

Birth cry

The new born infant's cry is one of the most memorable and penetrating sounds we can hear. Perhaps this is something that is a trigger for the most human of qualities, but also in terms of sheer noise it is quite something. The pitch ranges from 500 Hz (a bit higher than a violin A string) to 1,000-2,000 Hz, which is at the top end of what people can hear. It's shrill. As for the loudness, at about a foot away from a new born baby's mouth, their cry can hit 80-85 decibels. (from Ostwald, P. The sounds of Infancy. Developmental Medicine and Child Neurology, 1972, pp350-361) That's equivalent to a hefty sound coming from a trombone, and that's just the baby's first attempt at using their lungs.

There is something magic about that amount of power and the effort it takes to create it. Yes it is a matter of life and death to take that first breath, but still, we each did this once with nothing to go on. What if you and I are able to muster that sort of inspiration for other endeavours in our lives with all the experience and development that we have now?

What motivation feels like

There are the people who wake up without a clock, before the dawn and with the birds outside, while an inner monologue of possibilities runs like ticker-tape in their heads. From the moment they open their eyes, rainbows shoot out as their lungs are filled with invigorating, oxygen-rich air, and they may even seem to slightly smile with each exhale.

Really?!? This is certainly not typical, but at the height of motivation, there may be moments that make you feel this way. It is very difficult to define motivation adequately. Motivation is what happens when you turn on your inner engine of *yes*. It is the reason *why* someone does something, but developing your 'yes' has to come from within, and likening the feeling to the superhero image above is not too farfetched. When motivated, there is something other-worldly about the feeling. Motivated people often do things that are not explainable in terms of everyday routines and they persist in spite of someone else thinking their choice of task is not practical or asking them to 'see reason' (…as they should stop, and will probably fail…).

We cannot physically see motivation front of us, but it is strongly linked to something we can and do see: our projected future. By that I do not mean hocus-pocus fortune telling. This type of projecting forward is something we all do to some extent, and it is unique to humans. You can test this out if you have a pet at home. For example if you have a dog and point to something in the distance for the dog to look at, they look at you, but do not comprehend how to follow the imaginary line from your extended finger to the object you want them to see. You can try this with a cat, but honestly you wouldn't expect the cat to look where you want at the best of times. People can *look beyond* a simple point of a finger in a physical sense, and also we can look beyond the confines of the present circumstances and situation to think of possibilities and imagine ourselves doing them.

The images we project, and their accuracy and the likelihood of them becoming a reality depend on how well we can assess the current situation and environment, analyse the components, understand our own current capabilities, as well as understanding aspects of the intended arrival point, and something of the path between here and there. When there is belief in the *possibility* of what could be, and of what you could do or achieve, hope is born and motivation follows. This belief in the possibility is your self-efficacy, but not self-efficacy as originally defined as relating to an immediate criterial context, this is a projected self-efficacy: '*I believe I will be able to…*' and you may have the belief without all the details of the specific situation.

The facts of reality and dreams of a projected future often clash. How can now coincide with a different then? The endless treading water of optimism is not helped if we are weighed down by the grim details of reality. In reality there is great suffering in the world, and if we focus on that it can easily overcome us. Optimism is not realism, and having this enduring drive, the belief that fuels motivation requires us not to focus on the negative. As I write this the world is swept with corona virus, and surely the doctors, down to every person needs to focus on the positive possibility rather than letting the very real statistics and probability of how easy it is for a single person to spread the disease drag us down. There needs to be hope to maintain the energy to think and do, and your self-efficacy – the belief that you can – is the foundation of it all.

A simple image that comes to mind is the English Bumble Bee. These gentle creatures are between the size of a large marble and a ping pong ball, huge and fluffy. A common misconception is to say they shouldn't be able to fly. They do look ridiculous as they amble close to the ground and land on some small weak flower, nearly toppling the plant as they do their bee thing. They fly, using the world's magnetic field to guide their seemingly aimless direction, and they somehow on their already big bodies, gather up to 90% of their bodyweight in pollen. These individual tiny (well big when you come across one) creatures keep bumbling and flying, defying all the people who say they can't and shouldn't, and actually they do. They spend all their time literally smelling the flowers in a way that is completely essential to our ecosystem.

An exercise in possibilities

The first step in maintaining this positivity and being able to project forward involves learning to be present in the here and now. In Chapter 1 we discussed awareness. Put some of that into practice and take a moment to consider your awareness of the things around you. Could you describe your current setting? Could you describe it in detail? Visually, when we perceive, our brains map the world around us. Once this map is created, our conscious awareness actively focuses on a small stream of new information to keep that map up to date, and most everything else is interpolated from previously observed information, and lots is ignored. To explain this simply, imagine an early cartoon. The background is static, as it was all hand drawn, and only one or two characters or details in the foreground move. We are interested in the change. Our brains pick up change, and just like those animations, our consciousness allows the unchanged things to remain and not take up active perceptive energy.

What does this have to do with optimism or motivation? Optimism is not realism. Realism states what is, whereas optimism looks to what could be. Our mind's habit of awareness looks to assess the present and be ready to react. For example, as I drive my car, I see the road, with its markings, and the houses and driveways and trees. They all go by like a repeated, single-frame cartoon background. Partly this allows us to get on with the task of driving and focus our attention where we need it. When there is an unexpected change, like a ball rolls out into the road, as a driver my attention is suddenly drawn to the ball and I react by hitting the breaks and stopping my car. Reactions are important, and our brains look out for change, which is good. However, reactions are not the drivers of innovation. The driver of innovation is the unseen possibility that lies dormant, existing quietly before a reaction is needed. By being actively aware of our settings, our physical and mental interpersonal situations, we can both notice and question all sorts of things: What we see, how we are, what we do, how we fit, what can be, and this awareness is the first step to realising possibilities that will align with our self-efficacy beliefs and motivate us. Actively noticing before change happens means moving beyond the default (the easiest mental load) of banking information until we need to alter our course to react, and instead we are able to see the things right in front of us in a new light and there is a possibility they can take on new meaning.

If you were to shut your eyes now and   describe your surroundings, could you? What level of detail would you be able to include? Sounds? Textures? Feel of things? Experiential details? There's something to being allowed to consciously experience in a sensational way, and then we begin to access some of those otherwise untapped connections and possibilities.

Just for a minute, look around you and consider some part of the place where you are that 'just is', whether it's a plain white wall or a shelf with intricately arranged nick-knacks. If you are in a different than normal setting, had you noticed it before? If it's a place you know well has it always been like that? How could it be different? Why would you want it different? If you don't want it different, what would happen if it was changed? What would be the impact? How would it make you feel? Thinking this way may be something completely new to you. Entertaining what might seem like random questions can lead you to consider possibilities.

You may have noticed I didn't qualify or judge the possibilities. I didn't say good or bad or cast any directive of should, but instead simply asked the questions. Thinking widely is a skill that is not part of everyone's daily routine. It is one thing to think within the parameters that we already know, but how can you know beyond what you know?

It would be foolish to suggest you can know the

unknown, but you can perceive what is around you now, and you can learn to understand the possible interactions with the things and people in your current setting. Through understanding these, and practicing your skills, you can become better at connecting A to B, and then when working toward C or D, the application of what you do know is less far-fetched.

Vision: The dreamer within

There are immediate and conscious limits to understanding everyday practical situations. For example: *There are oats in the cupboard, so I can add water/milk to make porridge, but I am not likely to make a pie with them.* Yet there are very deep and complex pathways that we hold in our brains made of all our different experiences throughout life that very often are not accessed and perhaps not even consciously known of at all. For example, I might not make a pie with the oats, but I have seen cooking shows, seen documentaries about life in distant, rural communities, seen people use grains to make foods. If I was more aware of this potential library of information in my memories and from experiences of reading, watching, doing, then I might have more of a vocabulary for projecting the what *could be*. I could make the oats into flour and make a tasty pancake with very little effort. Admittedly pancakes are not pies, but they are also not porridge. There are options and possibilities if you allow yourself to have vision.

Ideally vision comes from within. Although if we do not have our own ideas now, someone can share their inspiration with us, whether through watching or listening to someone else. If we can learn to see – and dream – for ourselves, then possibilities suddenly expand. The capacity to dream is within us, and like every skill it needs to be consciously developed, and importantly, it needs to be allowed to exist. The idea of allowing ourselves to project forward beyond what we can see now, and dream will be discussed more in the section on barriers. We can learn to hone and use our capacity to project and dream and then work to grow and move progressively toward these goals. As we do this, our self-efficacy is very important. Self-efficacy beliefs sustain us in the tasks we do now, and also they are applied about what we believe about our capabilities for the future.

As we iteratively work toward the dream, the vision, we begin a process of constantly checking, taking an active awareness of our selves and our surroundings, noticing and orienting our understanding, and assessing our self-beliefs about each situation. We have self-efficacy for the present, each task we undertake, and self-efficacy for our progress toward out goals. Careful use of strategies and making the most of the tools and opportunities around us helps us progressively work toward achievement and goals.

Learning how to dream takes time, and nobody can be expected to grow a new leaf to turn over instantly. The plants have that unstoppable urge to grow, and they hold in them the potential for wonderful growth. When first looking at the sprout of a seed, it hardly looks like unfurled leaves, and even less like a flower. Growth takes time, and learning to carve our own paths takes belief from us, a willingness to change and move forward, despite unknowns, and care.

Barriers, limitations, and blockages

With the best intentions in the world, it is not possible simply to set out to learn perception, awareness, to have vision and dream, and then enact your capabilities through successful actions. Inevitably there will be bumps in the road. Sometimes we can see what these are, and other times it is something of a mystery even when the answer is staring right back at us.

My own dang self

When I look in the mirror, sometimes for whatever reason I don't see anything at all. I don't *see* myself, let alone realize my capabilities or how I could plan and achieve my goals. In daily life I just do what I have to from one moment to the next, the things I need to do, what I'm told to do. In essence, I am in a cage - my own cage. All of the good ideas presented in this book and elsewhere in the wider world to do with change and growth ultimately have come from within, and if sometimes like me, you feel like are in a cage, this presents a real challenge in terms of finding a sense of *yes*. - at least for that moment anyway.

Wherever you are now, on the sofa, in a car, on top of the world, this is where you begin. The setting, the space and place are easier to name than how you fit within it. Starting with these details, allows you to begin to build the puzzle, and small bits of how you interact with what is around you will begin to form a picture of your now. This is like the above exercise recognising the nick-knacks and then considering *what if?* By first allowing ourselves to notice the surroundings, we can then look at ourselves and ask that same what if. Anyone's self is complex, and only you can look inside and know your particular situation – with all the past has shown, given, or dragged you through, your skills, dreams, failures, and successes, the people you like, who make you laugh, and those you pass by and never knew. When you consider your what ifs, you will be looking at a couple of the mirror tiles on that complex disco ball of **you**, and as you look and that silvery ball turns there may be a particular something that just catches your minds eye.

When you catch a glint and see a bit of you that you hadn't seen before, that is a moment of meaning – catching your own eye in that mirror, and this time someone looked back. Once we recognize ourselves, we can address where we are and begin to think about what we can do. The understanding of our selves is crucial to being able to notice, think, and believe – yes, that's the beginning of self-efficacy. Then we have agency. We grow.

That is all hard work. There's no soft way to put it. Physical labour is one thing, and the mental stuff is another level. There is no obvious external deadline to meet, no tangible reward for doing this, and no practical way to measure how far you've come and where you have yet to go. It would be so much simpler if it was like doing the dishes. See something that needs cleaning, pick it up, put it in the sink, add soap, turn on the water, scrub, drain, and dry. All tidy! Each step has clear instructions that work for all sorts of dishes after any kind of meal, and it is really obvious when you have done each thing. Other people can recognize your progress and if it's your job to do the dishes, you probably even get paid. Personal growth and self-efficacy and agency are not like that. It is all about moving beyond, and a lot of people are complacent with simply going from today to tomorrow, with a few commercials in between. Be the person who changes the channel.

Stepping beyond the past

There are two things: we can know and we can dream. We can know the past and the present, but the future is yet to be. That sounds so obvious. It is far easier and more concrete to wrap our minds around the past. Like reading a storybook, the words are already on the page, and we've been there. The present is more difficult as words are *being* written moment by moment, and not everyone either realizes they may be the ones actually writing their own words, or they cannot keep pace with reading and understanding what someone else is writing, as it happens in real time. Thinking that image through, even the idea of writing the present and reading the past takes effort to see and understand. That effort, the process, is what engagement with the present feels like and simply being *here* takes focus, energy, and a willingness to keep at it. There's no standing still or sitting down, as the present keeps being the present – now, now, now. It is active and there is no security in the present like there is in the past.

Engaging in the present means a willingness to dip your toe into the unknown. The future holds unknowns, and this is obvious, but the present too is all new with its constant unfolding moments of now. These moments are where possibilities lay. The people who cling to the comfort of facts already written down do not like the risk of uncertainty in the present, and certainly not that of the future. They do not think in terms of projecting forward, but live in a time that is already decided, where they can know, accept, and be confident in the security of known facts.

Once we commit to stepping beyond the concept of the past, this is a move toward being present, but living this way is not something we simply decide to *do*. Although, the decision to put one foot in front of the other is an important one, and necessary, people have a lifetime of past that they have also walked through. Life deals us each experiences that we may carry with us. Some of these will be wonderfully formative and cherished, whereas others can be heavy burdens. As with an unseen self-cage, many may not even know they carry the weight of the past. Unloading this baggage is neither trivial nor easily explainable in the space of these pages, though I can acknowledge that each of us has encountered people, places, and things in our lives that have marked us in various ways. Speaking for myself, learning to recognize what has impacted me and my life and to accept the positive and unpick negative moments and relationships so they are not metaphorical knots left in my hair has taken anywhere from days to decades. It is important to recognize that we are each on our own personal road: I am not you. You are not that other person. We are each someone, with our own experiences and our own dreams. Nobody can take the good or relieve you of the difficulties of the past, nor can anyone understand it for you. These are things you will do in your own time, and throughout life you will always have your dreams.

Blindness of privilege and living in an imbalanced world.

Think back to all the times someone asked you to do something, big or small, did you ever without really thinking, simply reply with, *'No, I can't do that'*?

Perhaps your 'no' was in response to a request for help with something they were doing, or maybe they were airing a clever plan for you, like starting a challenging new project, or maybe it was just a task you didn't feel like doing. I'm sure, whether in response to a trivial question or a life-changing proposition, we will all have said *no, I can't do that* at some point in time. Why though? Was it because of the question? Why would you have said no just like that, without giving it a second thought? Was there something about that task? There could be any number of reasons that came to mind for you. I can think of a thousand reasons for not doing things I consider annoying, like cleaning the drains, filing papers, or sorting photographs – oh photographs! There are countless places in my household across various electronic devices where untold repositories of images live that are not tagged, downloaded, or saved anywhere except maybe on that device. My mind groans: *who has the time to sort that- not me!?*

I can't is a wonderfully vague, yet firm statement. It can cover a lot of ground in the same way that a shrug of the shoulders conveys a clear statement of non-engagement with the task or activity and all the thought processes that go along with it while avoiding giving any specific reason for why. *Can't* is a closed door, and chances are the argument (if there is one at all) for saying can't has at least a few holes in it. Sometimes we say *can't* when there are other possibilities that we have not yet explored. It is easier to refuse and say something is simply not possible than to find a way to figure it out. This is not a suggestion that we should never say no. There are many times in our lives when we indeed want to and should say no. It is also very possible to correctly say *no, I won't*, and to fully realize that you do have the capability to do whatever that task is. We just need to think it through.

The reasons for an answer of *can't* might be something you perceive as beyond your control, like a physical life-fact: I can't go outside without my oxygen tank. It would be silly to refute that and pretend that actually if you believed in yourself you could somehow magic away a condition. There are some things, qualities and characteristics in our lives, that are genuinely boundaries and indeed barriers that limit what we have access to doing. I say perceive not to suggest that anyone is dreaming up a condition, these are real and those who do not have similar boundaries need to think more widely to begin to both understand and to enable others access to opportunities. The idea of mentioning perception is because there is often a way to allow engagement. Simply because someone or their situation is different does not mean they *can't*.

Consider how the world changed in early 2020. As the COVID19 virus moved through the population, people needed to change their pattern of living. Suddenly, many able-bodied people across the world found their movements restricted: they were house-bound for months. Social and work patterns changed dramatically. For some people who perhaps already had a condition that prevented them moving about easily, their daily lives had already been mainly inside, well *before* this virus came into the world. The able-bodied population was forced (unknowingly) to experience and look at the world and life through this different lens. On social media, the immediate reaction was a cry of *I can't do this, my life as I know it is gone...* and there was a general sense of doom and gloom.

A few weeks into this period of restriction, something happened showing me an unexpected glimpse of yes. Someone I know who indeed is officially classed as 'disabled' and does have difficulty moving around was one of those people who in the past often replied with *I can't* to suggestions of *'why don't you do this...?'* This person said to me, out of the blue, *'I'm going to take a class at Yale.'*

?!?!?

I stopped in my tracks.

Besides being a wonderful thing to do, whether at a university, the library, via an app, or in the garden (when someone decides to learn I do a little happy dance), this sudden declaration made me think and re-think. The whole world was put into a similar situation to this person for the first time, and instead of seeing a closed door and announcing that life had ended like most people, she somehow saw an opportunity. Was this because the playing field was equalized for the first time? I will never know. However, because people were forced to think within these newly imposed limitations of social distancing and closed physical premises, they came up with creative possibilities for accessibility and continuation of learning. Sometimes the limitations that impact us and our perception of what we can do are not actually firm walls, but rules, ways of working, or a lack of awareness and consideration by others for the situation we have.

Sometimes, as well, we do set our own boundaries, imposing limitations where there genuinely are none. Think back to my asking the question *why* did you say *'no, I can't…'*. This may have been because of self-created boundaries that are not actually impossible to navigate, but it is easier to say they are than to face them and either dismantle the imaginary wall or work around whatever limitations do exist.

If you can think back to when restrictions on social movement impacted your life, these were not imagined or self-created, but were an imposed barrier. They were not insurmountable, but working with them and overcoming them required effort, creativity, endurance, and a lot of belief that despite it all, there is still a way to find that yes. People had to go beyond their initial reactions and assumptions about what tasks could be done and how to carry these out. Those who found their yes learned to be open to new possibilities.

Where barriers are not perceived and need to be

When driving on the road and you come upon some roadworks or construction, this is always clearly labelled. It is easy to recognize and follow the signature orange cones, fresh reflective paint, and portable flashing lights marking exactly where the problem is and guiding cars to steer clear and change their direction. In life it seldom happens that everyday activities are marked out carefully for us in real time so we can navigate challenges via the best and safest path. Often there are no obvious signs to see and unlike the road, there would be no *thing* to mark anyway. Part of developing awareness and perception is learning to see things that aren't physically there.

People's thoughts, attitudes, behaviours, and societal norms all impact us and the way we live. For example the restrictions imposed on people's movement in an effort to reduce the spread of the COVID virus are not observable in the same as a row of potted plants on a window sill. Nobody can pick up social distancing and examine it. A restriction or directive is not a thing you can see at all, but you can see the ripples of implications it causes on actions and outcomes. The concrete repercussions may be visible, however waiting to see these manifest as a result from an unseen barrier is too late to notice them. Think about the simple directive to 'stay home'. Not leaving the house has both far and near consequences, but not everyone sees them until they happen. If these are only realized when opening the cupboard to find you are out of pasta or flour, without having realized staying at home would disrupt the usual pattern of going out to get food or shopping whenever there's a need, that's a problem. We can't see the restriction, but no food on a plate is something you can (and don't want to) see. How can we beat something we can't see? There is a need to mentally play out the scenario, like a chess player does. Chess players are particularly known for being prepared; they know both what game they are playing and are very well acquainted with the rules and all the possibilities.

Sometimes we do not know what game is on the table, let alone all the rules, and not all life situations can be explained in such stark practical terms. Far more often than not there are unseen barriers in our daily lives that evade our conscious awareness. Without thinking or realising we carry out our lives despite without realising we adapt to compensate as if the obstacle was never there. Take how you are sitting as an example. At least someone reading this will be sitting cross-legged (and if not now, chances are you have sat this way before, so you can imagine it). Crossing one leg over the other produces an unnatural kink in the spine, and in order to support this very common, yet awkward and stressful posture, muscles in our back compensate so we do not notice the imbalance, and we suppress the feelings of pain resulting from the imposed spinal twist. Because of our learned and practiced compensation, we hardly know this obstacle exists. We not only willingly tolerate it but we often actually choose to engage with it. We regularly and actively compensate to allow this behaviour to continue.

Barriers, obstacles, and roadblocks can be restrictions we create or perpetuate for ourselves, but these can also can be external: imposed by those around us, implicitly part of societal infrastructure, or designed into our physical settings. It is quite likely that we may not even realize they exist.

Where there is a societal imbalance, it needs to be noticed. In society privilege causes imbalance. Sometimes the way to deal with it is not immediately obvious and may seem insurmountable. Just as with our learned habits, we also compensate for restrictions that are not inherent to our physical selves. Those who are not in a position of privilege are forced to compensate if they want to achieve the same as someone else – whether this involves walking farther, working earlier or later, going through the red tape that someone else could step over. The effort of keeping up, treading water with others who seem to float on by, takes a toll and gathering the energy and conviction to focus, looking both outward and inward to examine and perceive what the imbalance is, is necessary. When we look and are perceptive, someone or something will show us a glimpse of that difference, and then we can begin to recognize what it is.

That moment of recognition is a watershed. Metaphorically we move from treading water to having the vision of the possibility of stepping out onto dry land and maybe even having the choice to swim more or walk away. Whether we can actually *do* this or not, is not the important thing at this stage. One step is to recognize the imbalance for whatever it is. The decisions that we can then make, or any future actions depend on our individual settings, both mentally and physically. It may be that a change of perspective is all we need to start making a change, or there might be serious planning that takes time, and many layers of action necessary before we feel able to move forward.

Although this can seem like it takes a super-human effort, the willingness to see and seek understanding, explanation, and answers is paramount. Even in the most wonderful situation, there is always change and change means a shift in balance. Complacency and an unawareness will perpetuate imbalance whereas the motion of perceptive questioning will act as a check to mediate and work toward a fluid state. When you walk or run, the body is constantly shifting, falling from one foot to the other and catching itself, yet with skilful coordination you feel secure and can maintain a level gaze focused on whatever you like.

Now what?

Creating infrastructure for REAL GROWTH

In our modern lives, we have become accustomed to convenience, and people don't always have to learn or even look for a way to do things that might be challenging. Society has worked to automate, simplify, and create space to enable people ease and leisure time, where a century ago we would have *had* to work or had to figure things out for ourselves. Today there are gadgets to do many things for us. The very nature of *auto*matic means something is done for us. When done for us, where is our agency in the process? Without an active part in the thinking, knowing, and doing, we cannot foster growth.

The reliance on technology and instant solutions in our lives means people are used to looking outward to source answers. Reaching out can be a great tool if that means networking to seek information or expertise, but not if you are simply shopping for a quick fix. Societal mechanisms, social media and advertising teach people to expect something.

'Lose weight now, buy… Need cash? Call... Download our newest app… Want success? Enrol now in this easy course… You can look your best, just…'

Fabricated norms as portrayed by television and social media entice with a sense of what could be and even suggest an entitlement for people to do, have, or be a certain way. Anything you can think of can be done to you, done for you, browsed, bought, or delivered to your door. However, the growth that dissolves barriers to open pathways is not another Lego brick added on to the tower, or an external accessory like a backpack full of books. That's not adding knowledge but carrying weight.

Think back to the plant that keeps growing. What does this take? In practical terms it takes sunlight, soil, and water. Too much and the plant will drown, bake, or be buried, and that's not good. With the elements come complications of extra factors like the wind. Factors interact: riding on the wind, the water is delivered through the rain, sometimes falling gently and other times pelting the plant. Even though the plant thirsts for the water, the rain can be harsh and damaging to its young leaves. We experience the same. There are things we need, but we cannot simply have them made to order; it's complicated. Growth takes internalisation, digestion, it uses our energy as we turn food into thought and form new strength, muscles, and ideas. We must use ourselves, actively engage in doing, stretching both our minds and bodies, and all this takes time.

If you have ever grown carrots, you will know they are both hearty and particular. Admittedly a carrot is not a person, but it does deal with a rock in the soil by growing around it, sometimes into quite silly shapes. Carrots do not let the rocks stop them. Perhaps the carrot could find a way to remove the rocks, but a practical solution is to grow around it. Whether to divert or dismantle whatever barrier comes our way, we need to build up strength and resilience so when the way is clear, we can move forward.

Once we understand our surroundings and difficulties, as people and not carrots, we can plan and construct mechanisms to monitor change and progress. Reflection is necessary, both our own perspective and a wider view. Importantly this is not something we need to do alone. Especially if there is an imbalance and not simply a barrier, we need to have a sort of temperature gauge, whether a person, place, space, or time, and using external references can help to orient and reorient us with every step we take.

Looking beyond boundaries

I travelled with a gal who would occasionally say *'It is what it is'*, and I remember when she would say that, kind of looking at her funny, like hmmm, well did you just say 'etc.' That is one of those words people use when they can't think of any other words to say, or like a comic of the world from a dog's point of view where the people think and talk, but only say 'woof'. In my mind I think- yes indeed, it is what it is, and also- absolutely not, you have hardly taken the time to look at all.

Whatever the task in front of you, whether real or dreamed, from chopping firewood, to being a civic leader, working in a tall building, leading a team of people across the globe, inventing something, baking a cake, raising a child, to whatever is in your mind's eye, none of these things are beyond any of us. Perhaps they are not instantly accessible, but they do not belong only to a privileged few and not to you or me. Plenty of people will, however, tell you that you really should or should not do something, and some will go as far as saying specifically that you can or can't do something. In reality **nobody** can tell you what you can or can't do. Externally defining capabilities that are by definition *yet to be* realized makes no logical sense. Only you can judge and decide what your capabilities are further, and you are the one to decide whether you believe in them. Only you can have self-efficacy to do things; people cannot give it to you or take it from you. Choosing the path, looking at what is there, and working around or through roadblocks is all part of enacting your self-efficacy. You can be influenced; there is bound to be traffic, weather, and unforeseen things-debris, birds, glare, and the way you deal with these is up to you. You are in the driver's seat. Self-efficacious people are far more likely to be persistent and resilient in what they do, and to get results.

Looking beyond takes vision. Some of us are inspired to grow, but another impetus for change is necessity. Early 2020 witnessed the world's action and reaction to barriers in new ways. Lots changed to enable people to look beyond the threat, but the looking beyond that happened, at least initially, was based on understanding facts analytically and clinically to maximize a reaction to stop and prevent further harm. The situation was rather like fighting a fire. I wouldn't consider that a recipe for personal growth. When necessity causes change, it is only when we have a moment to stand back and reflect that we can see. One of my long-time school friends volunteered as an emergency worker in Los Angeles during the peak of the 2020 crisis, and in regard to the rapid changes made by society and individuals, she said:

"What was implausible a few months ago is now not only possible but happening; let's not forget that when in the future something is deemed impossible.
It's not about going back to how it was - it's always been about making it better."
Anji Gaspar-Milanovich, 4 April, 2020

What Anji unintentionally demonstrated so well, is an example of what having vision and allowing ourselves access to that wider perspective of possibilities gives. The benefit of vision is it allows us time for introspection and consideration, whereas change by necessity comes when there is danger or comforts have been stripped away, leading to solution-oriented thinking where the solution is survival instead of growth.

It is what it is, or is it? Let's say *it* is a cup and it has water in it. I could notice that. I could see the water or I could see the emptiness, or I could see the curve of the glass. Facts are part of knowing and understanding how to look beyond. How I see it goes beyond the glass to acknowledge the refinement of the craftsmanship, the time it took to learn the skills, the way the artisan made just that shape, and how it feels in my hand now. It *is,* but also it is so much more. Having vision is not about living in fallacy by inventing false truths or rewriting the reality around us. Vision does require we have one foot firmly planted in reality, recognising and understanding the facts, and the other foot steps out into the air. This is our projecting forward. That idea sounds challenging in terms of thinking and concepts, but every time we walk from one place to another we do this. Standing still is not a productive option and dragging our feet will not get us much of anywhere. We maintain a balance in the motion of walking, with one foot connected to the ground in fact and reality, and the other foot is our enacted vision. Leaving the tether of the ground, it demonstrates the forward projection of optimism and possibility. Balance is achieved when we do not tie ourselves completely to living only in facts but also in dreamed possibility. This is the basis for a constructive framework.

Understanding the facts is fundamental to accurately assessing the reality of any situation we are in; we need to know the soil, the road, the things that surround us in life. Once we see what *is* then we can look beyond. If you can detect a hole ahead, recognize and understand its properties, this gives you a start to use your physical and cognitive tools to devise a way around. Doing the prep work to lay out the cones and markers, creates a framework of appropriate guidance so when it comes time to walk you can go for it.

When people put up boundaries, create infrastructures around you, look for their limit. If they build a fence, *hop the fence*. Whether a small decorative Box hedge, picket fence, or something meant to be more restrictive, our thinking has to be that there is a way around it, above it, beyond it. Thinking through processes, knowing you have the skills and realising your belief, unlocks agency. Once you learn to see what's around you when standing still and begin to adopt the optimistic stance of walking forward, you can dare to dream – of running, swimming, even flying. Being aware of and owning your self-efficacy beliefs makes all the difference.

Go on, hop the fence.

The good thing loop

I see, I know, I feel, I do.
I am, I can.
I see, I know, I feel, I do.
I am, I can....

The good thing loop is a cycle, but not like day and night, seasons of the year, life and death, it is more like the perpetual cycle of how the sun feeds itself. Once the ingredients are there and we know the right formula, the components are there to fuel billions of years of daylight. That loop is a good thing. For something closer to home, think of a tree that keeps sprouting new leaves as it grows new branches. It becomes more full. Each of the tasks in our life, whatever we turn our attention and energies to, is like growing another leaf.

I see

This is about awareness and perception, and by now its importance is clear. Everyday we can challenge what we take in from the physical cues around us.

Knowing what you believe is fundamental to learning. It

sounds obvious but it is a tangible skill to recognize what you see, and this conscious understanding of the what and how allows us to process connections. People see, hear, feel, and experience all the time, but often they are not aware of what crosses their path: What they have, do, how they interact, how subtle thoughts and actions or non-actions reinforce habits or ignore new possibilities. Knowing involves intellectually realising and acknowledging our experienced reality.

I know

This knowing and thinking takes effort and because of that, some people just don't do it; they don't think. Many people do think and still do not actively know and understand because they fail to engage with the metacognitive aspects of awareness. Paying attention to the intricacies of how we notice can give insight into the potential influence and role the different things and events can play in the tasks we do.

As a really clear example. If you put a glass of water in front of me, it means nothing if I do not realize what it is and what I can do with it. I also have to understand how to get that water from the glass to inside me. Can I just pick it up and drink it? Are there any complications? Are there other people sitting at the table also wanting that glass of water? Maybe my hands are tied and I cannot simply pick up the glass and drink it. Can I gulp it down or do I need to eek it out? I need to think in order to process the whole situation. A surface glance may be my norm, but just seeing the thing in front of me is not really enough.

If people *knew* what there was around them, how they fit, and what was involved with whatever they intended to do, so much more would and could happen. The explicit mapping of the 'what is' to the potential, the possibility of 'what could', and knowing how these relate sets people up for the next step: to feel.

I feel

Feeling has multiple levels of meaning in terms of its role in this loop. On one level feeling is the everyday emotional response that does not need any technical or formal explanation. If you like strawberries and you see a plate of them, you look and get excited. You feel the anticipation of having that nice treat. If there is a spider dangling from the ceiling and that scares you, you know that too, and your feeling translates into an unplanned physical and mental reaction. There are all sorts of physical mechanisms, chemical and neurological, that can be cited to explain how feeling is manifest, but I am quite happy to keep it with an everyday response that ranges from a smile to a shriek to a sigh. Those sorts of feelings are yours, and do not need to be explained for this cycle.

Another type of feeling has to do more specifically with self-efficacy and is the result of examining whatever it is you are doing. For a visual effect, imagine you are the main character in a comic strip and when you 'examine' a task, it is visualized with lasers coming out of your eyes and scanning the task (even if the task is conceptual, go with me here). The comic might look like this:

You ask yourself, 'How do I feel about walking up that hill?'
  (pause)
  think
  LASERS SHOOT OUT OF YOUR EYES AT THE HILL.

Yep, now I know how I feel, **and that's** *your* **self-efficacy.**

I do. I am. I can.

The last stage of the good thing loop is the most outwardly visible. You do (the task). You do it because you have the conviction, the self-efficacy in yourself, and at that point there is assurance both of what you *are* (self) and of what you *can do* (capabilities).

This active stage is not simply played out as a matter of course, because our self-efficacy is influenced by external and internal factors. Theoretically our past experience should be the greatest influencer on our beliefs, but the strength and effectiveness of the different influences depends on our subjective relationship to them.

Sometimes in a situation, a lesser influence actually impacts us most, more than a past experience. For example have you ever done something that you knew you had failed at before, but someone you really respected and trusted told you that you could do it, and for some reason you believed them and did it? That hardly makes logical sense but it happens. When you keep falling off your bike and your brother looks you in the eye to say, I know you can do this, you listen. Perhaps on a deeper level you know that he has already done it; he can ride his bike, and this in conjunction with his reassurance overrides the fact that you know you consistently fall off.

For me when this happens, it feels like the one influence that comes to the surface in that moment is strongly linked with what I perceive as most valued then. With the bike example it might be: *If you are willing to believe in me, then I can make the jump to believe in myself too.* Sometimes validating the underlying 'thing' we value most- even if we do not have a name for it and couldn't put a finger on it to identify exactly what *it* is. This sense of value allows us to own the influence.

The influences on self-efficacy retain their order: e.g. firstly mastery/doing a task, second is observing the task, next is being persuaded you can do the task, and lastly come the physical signs and thoughts from yourself, *as long as you value and recognize each influence in that order.* Then you own the processes as they occur, and it makes sense that they influence you. Just as it is possible to look at something and neither see nor recognize it, this is also true with the potential influences on self-efficacy. How can something you do not know or recognize have a deeper influential power over you and your self-efficacy beliefs? As long as we do see, recognize, and feel, then doing (or traditionally called 'mastery') is still the ultimate benchmark by which we affirm our self-efficacy beliefs.

Completing this cycle can be very motivating, especially when we keep actively engaged in each step. Once the last part is finished and we have completed doing our task, we go back to the beginning and start again with seeing. You might look for evidence, asking, *'Did I do it?'* It is completely natural to seek confirmation from both external and internal sources. This element of reflection deepens our awareness and adds to our palate of tools for the future. Each time we complete the cycle we learn slightly more about ourselves, strengthening the sense of *I am* and *I can.* It is indeed a good thing loop.

CHAPTER FIVE
Learning and You

Our relationship with LEARNING

Nearly all of us will have been taught by someone in school, but how many of us knew how to learn? In grade school I remember being taken out of class every day to go to some special class – there were only five of us from across two year groups I think – it's a bit hazy as it was 5th grade. We were taken to a small room where a jovial Mrs Bailey, who even then we thought looked young, taught us how to think both critically and creatively. What on earth happened to the other 50 children in our year? Were they supposed to magically know how to learn? I cannot imagine that learning spelling lists and doing reading comprehension exercises was enough and it is not clear that any of us really knew how to learn.

Today it is more possible than ever to both access information and teach yourself a wide variety of skills. From organized online classes to individual online videos and podcasts, there is no shortage of instruction at our fingertips. Libraries of information in all sorts of formats exist and are accessible. Especially as has been seen with the onset of COVID-19 and a period of social distancing, knowing how to find things and what to do with the information you find can be crucial to even the understanding of what is possible, and definitely to the success of someone's learning.

And with teachers

A good teacher acts as a guide, someone who already has the foresight to see a path and perhaps know enough about it to tell you a few interesting things. They can help you to notice, warn you when a bend or uneven bit is coming, and can even steady you if you stumble. I say *a* path because it may not be *the* path that is your dream goal in life and completely individually tailored to you.

Teachers in formal education settings are often bound by school or government required curricula, that can specify everything from content, to methods of teaching and testing, and they may not have the freedom or resources to readily adapt to every student's unique aspirations. (Not all students know what their aspirations are either) Some teachers do have the freedom to teach as they like, and even those who have more restrictions imposed upon them can still encompass the set curriculum and plant the seeds to go beyond it, allowing the creative pursuit of plans and projects. However, this takes effort and not every teacher does reach out - sometimes there are teachers who do teach by the book, and once you, as a student, are trained to jump those textbook hoops, people may well pat you on the back and tell you how well you're doing on that step-by-step path, and that it is indeed your path. They might be right, or maybe not.

Personally I would not like to think that a textbook written a year or two or ten ago somehow knows exactly what and how I should be doing now. That does not mean it is useless; you can still learn a lot from a teacher who teaches by the book, the key is to know how to learn. If you understand how to get the most out of the situation, the useful knowledge, skills, experience, then you can follow that step-by-step, already planned out curriculum that is intended to be a definitive path (even though you do not intend to take that path at all in your life), and you can smile knowing that you can confidently and comfortably walk through the steps for that course curriculum, and *afterwards,* when you walk out of the door you will both have some extra skills and knowledge and be free to take the pieces you want, leave the others behind, and choose your own course of action. When you know how to learn you can effectively pave your own path.

Before getting to that stage most people rely on teachers. This is ok except for one startlingly obvious point. At what point in our lives do we actually have teachers? The most obvious answer is in formal education settings:

"Welcome class, my name is Miss Rabbit / Mr Jeffers / Sam (for those rebel teachers who just use a first name) and I'll be your teacher this year."

We certainly do have teachers outside and after formal education, but they appear in a different guise. They seldom have the tell-tale signs many associate with the classic teacher. For example, they probably do not have a desk or office or stand in front of a class, and what about assigning homework or giving grades? My guess is nope. None of these. The fact that these are missing may be a very good thing. Some of these things help us, but sometimes they tell us things in ways that mean we do not do the thinking for ourselves.

We too are different around those who teach us in what may be less identifiable settings in life. Somehow we don't come to learning in the same way as when sitting behind a desk. In formal settings, people submit to teachers both literally and figuratively. Students do what they are told, as a matter of course, and seldom question either why or whether whatever they have been directed to do is a good idea or useful for them. Asking is good; questioning is good;

blind submission to someone's authority is not so good. A positive aspect of having a healthy learning relationship is trust: the lowering of barriers. In formal education settings people are expected to take on new things when they learn, and that is not always easy or obvious. Students who trust their teacher does have some sense of vision and good intentions to offer guidance based on knowledge and experience will be more willing to welcome the teacher's suggestions and then they can explore a path forward.

Beyond education settings we do not readily recognize people in our lives as teachers, or even as people to learn from, and that type of trust students can bestow on teachers that allows them to embrace new experiences is often guarded when everyday normal social defences are up. We place boundaries to protect our self, defend our social standing, keep us keenly aware of any threat. We spend our energy on protective awareness instead of inquisition. Of course it is sensible to be aware and not sensible to blindly trust everyone, however there are potential teachers and teaching situations all around.

To grow we must be looking for them, people, situations, happenings, and perceive relevant pieces that relate to our puzzle so we can learn from whatever they have to offer us. This learning requires vulnerability. Even learning (to learn for yourself) can be daunting as we move from our known comforts to exploring the new and uncertain.

Glass on the beach

As a child it was a treat to go to the beach. I lived in the mid-west of America and the very occasional trips to see my grandparents in California were magic. The power of the water terrified me, but the lapping tide revealing small glints of shell or sand or what I thought was treasure fascinated me. I would walk for hours looking at tiny nothings, and every once in a while I'd pick up what looked like a translucent pebble, maybe it would be green or brownish, or if you were really lucky blue. These were rounded, smaller than an acorn but bigger than a kernel of corn. If you held them up to the sun, you could almost see light go through them, and sometimes there would be a shiny smooth bit, but mostly they were frosted all around their surfaces. They were my gems, and I had a little box where I kept these. I never really thought about their stories until now.

These were of course fragments of discarded bottles. When I was a child they could easily have been from any fizzy drinks (as bottles were very common in the early 80s) or from alcohol bottles – the more exotic colours coming from fancy spirit bottles or the like. Regardless of the type, someone – a real person - chose that bottle, held it, and also let it go, cast it away to let the sea take its course. The bottle was carried here, there, over waves and down depths, crashing into the shore onto rocks near piers and dragged countless times back and forth across the sand with the tide. It sounds a bit like the daily grind for some people, through the same repetitive motions, with hardly a breath of air.

In the end it took someone outside that usual grind to notice at all. So I was that small child, squatting on the sand, parents quite happy I was occupying myself, looking for these gems. I wonder what the bottle would say if someone told it that one day someone would search for it and cherish the smallest fragment as precious?

What we know - our knowledge, and what we notice – the way we process and understand, are both important to realize and synthesize. Otherwise our experience and our surroundings can wash over us. We become washed like glass on the beach.

> - I want to catch the sun and glisten.

Shaped

The underpinnings of guiding your own learning are not

rocket science, but this takes a definite drive, a belief that you can (self-efficacy), and a willingness to fail in the process. Nobody is going to go from being the bottle in someone's hand to radiantly beaming as an example of art in the Louvre, but we can act to influence what happens so we are not completely at the mercy of 'whatevs' happens just because that's the way it is. Some things do happen with predictable regularity, like the tide, that even the ancient King Cnut knew he couldn't stop. His story goes that his army thought he claimed to be all powerful, and to prove he was not he sent them into the Bosham harbour (which is very muddy and quite smelly) and ordered them to keep back the tide, a task at which they obviously failed. *Our lives* are not that.

We are not all powerful either, but we do have choices about what and how we do things. These choices and our perception of them is not without conscious thought. The bottle in the tide is a passenger on an unchosen path, submitting without recourse to the battery of events, but to shape our selves and our futures we need to be active agents. When we choose, there will be moments when we feel dragged through the mud, worn, and genuinely tired, but there will also be blissful times of being supported by our surroundings, and then the times we stand and look at how we have shaped and formed what is around us. These will flow, and there is no external constant to be achieved.

The balance of new skills, with mix of positive achievements and genuine setbacks that go with real learning, especially when we are not yet in command of something, is a challenge. The constant comes from a steadfast belief, the root that keeps feeding that plant despite adverse conditions. This is the yes I can. No matter what the world says, what others say, there must be first and foremost a core belief in yourself, and this reality is not something to achieve, but is something we each keep coming back to everyday.

Reliance on…

Simply having that self-efficacy belief in yourself is not enough – it is fundamental, but not the only thing that makes achievement, growth, and progress possible. We are each situated in the world. In the most basic sense, we are living, breathing, eating, sleeping beings and how we interact with one another and with our surroundings matters. Some aspects of life are genuine contingencies, necessities for our existence, like if I don't take time to eat or sleep, I know that sooner or later I will fall over. Food and rest are basic physical needs, but we also have things in our lives that we have become accustomed to having or doing and we rely on them to guide and inform us.

Others, the environment, and you

Patterns of things, people, places, and habits of what, when, and how we do things; these are our tide and sometimes they are calming, giving us a feeling of being nicely on course (whatever that means). Sometimes the surroundings become what feels like a necessary part of our doing things. They are what we know, they are what we use, they are how it works here, wherever each of us is. The gentle repetition of a daily routines can easily tick along without our noticing a few days become a week or a month, or even fall into years of the same patterns.

When we do break the routines of our patterns, there are often requisite things, places, or people that we have as our go-to, to help us. It makes me think of one of my children when they were young, always carrying around 'fluffy cloud' which was a blue, frayed cotton blanket. I'm not suggesting that people or places are good luck charms, but the familiarity of a setting can make the difference to your receptivity when embarking on new elements to do with a project or a goal. For example, midway through the semesters, one of my classes had to switch rooms unexpectedly, and the new space was completely different – where it was in the building, the layout, the change in lighting, and these details threw people. Not everyone could not simply carry on where we left off, but took time to get used to the space. They were distracted, unsettled, and it was surprising how much of a gateway the actual space was for learning. The same holds true of other spaces; consider the place where you work, and your home. We make associations between the place and the action that takes place there, for example home is where we rest, and work is designed for certain types of productivity and when these become confused, it can be difficult to break the resulting habits.

From a young age we are trained to behave certain ways in certain spaces, and although it is not a problem to be quiet in a library, a concert hall, or a playground, it would be a genuine challenge if someone not only jumped around in a playground but also in a restaurant or lecture hall. Are we so tied to the place that we do not entertain the possibility to do things differently? The space does not have to be something we are tied to, at least in our minds.

When the space becomes restrictive instead of a supportive construction for us, we certainly need to rethink. In the spring of 2020 when people were forced to stay at home under lockdown conditions, that global pause caused the external spaces in their lives, for home, work, study, play, personal projects, and social spaces all to be suddenly relocated to the same physical location. These did not all became one and the same, instead people had to learn to differentiate what and how they did things to separate thoughts and processes for what they once did in different spaces so they could still focus and 'do' the things in each of the different areas of their lives. Even in everyday life where there are not imposed restrictions on spaces, uprooting what we do in one place to a different space takes more preparation and adaptive skill when we are reliant on the space.

Imagine the cello student who plays well in the familiar room where they have their weekly music lesson, but they may take time to adjust to the new space of playing in a hall, even with no audience. Associations tied to the different spaces are powerful. The thought of an audience all looking on while you play might be either exciting or scary. Separating associations with the space from tasks will help them to be freed from a single setting. There are of course physical (in this case acoustic) characteristics that will occur with any change of venue, and these cannot be ignored. However, identifying what has changed, how it impacts the delivery of the task (pursuit of the goal), and then addressing these does add a layer to the task, but it is not necessary to add extra associative restrictions.

Limiting ourselves to thinking we can only perform in the hall is simply not true, and there will be a time when you may find yourself in an unsuspecting venue, perhaps someone's front room in their house, in a situation where the performance you give there is just as real as in a fancy hall. Whether figuratively, or if you are performing from home to an online audience of thousands, you make it real. Just like playing in the playground and not playing in the restaurant, there are things we assume because of convention or simply because someone told us we are not allowed to do that.

We can hold on to people too, in terms of feeling either that we need them for confidence and assurance or just allowing others to be the guiding force of what we do and when. The idea that if someone, whether teacher or friend, is there when you do something is sweet, but also indulgent and can be restrictive. Admitting that makes me squirm. It's not an easy one to acknowledge that someone else can provide positive feedback and give *added* assurance, but the main belief, the self-efficacy, comes from you.

How to learn?

Teachers teach, right? Well teachers show and guide and do their best to present the information that can become part of learning, but they can't learn for me. Chef can cook the food, but I have to do about twenty steps before I eat it. I have to know where to find that chef, get to the restaurant, book a table, sit down, order the food, wait, receive the food and eat it, and then pay and get back home. There is a lot in there, and at any given step I could go wrong or miss something. Having gotten as far as eating, I could unknowingly mix the salad and the soup and ruin the meal. There is also a lot that can go right, especially if I know how to do it. Importantly it is *me*; it is *you*; we are the ones who learn, no matter how well the teacher teaches. Five star Michelin teachers can still fall flat if I, as the customer, sit there and let the ice cream melt.

If it is me, and not the teacher after all, the question changes. It is not about the chicken or the egg. I am the chicken and I am the egg, and I simply need to understand how to break out of that shell for myself.

Learning is a little like that and it does make you sweat and can leave you exhausted and frustrated if you go at it in a way that does not yield the best results.

How to learn? Learning is an ever-shifting balance like

watering the plant. How thirsty is the soil? How dry are the roots, How much can the pot hold? How fast should the water pour? Should the water come from above, onto the leaves or should the plant be immersed? The answer will be different for each type of plant in a specific location on a given day. Learning is personal to you and you, as a person, are situated in your life and in the world. The short of it is there is no one way, no single number, place or product as an answer. This book is not an answer. It is what you do with and about it that matters.

The plant, like a sponge will soak up the water. We too soak up the things around us, sights, sounds, experiences, but we have seen that we can notice and choose to poise our perception in a way to funnel these streams of input. When we soak it up, we still have to process it. If I get in a tub of water, stand in a puddle, it does not quench my thirst. Even if I pour a jug of water at my open mouth, like in some post-touchdown Hollywood moment, I still need to *drink* the water. Sitting at a desk writing out times tables, tracing the outline of a map, reading the next paragraph aloud as the teacher goes around the room so everyone can take part in the story. These are all ways one can engage in learning, but similarly one can engage in the activity and not learn at all. I enjoy the patterns I make as the columns of numbers are created on my lined paper, lining up the ascending numbers vertically, and missing the actual times table itself. I feel the dent in the tracing paper as my slightly dull coloured pencil finds the place to draw a line, not noticing whether it is Egypt or Ecuador that I draw, and what that might mean. I enjoy the reading circle, not for the story, but because I hear the other people's voices. The sound of my friends washes over me and the story goes by the by. Just like pouring water over our heads, the 'stuff' of learning can be all around us, but if we do not take it in and digest it, there is no guarantee the experienced outcome will be anything like whatever was intended to be learned.

The 'how to' of learning is not obvious and if we do know how to learn then we can take something from every situation. Learning happens not by being simply exposed to or surrounded by stuff, but when we make it useful and meaningful for us. Each of us can develop a collection of strategies that works for us to unpick, dissect, expose, reveal, shine a light on, and find the meaning and relevance of whatever it is we are approaching. School experience is the obvious starting place to look for hints of these strategies, as that is when there is (was) both an allowance and expectation to encounter new things and to have explanations provided of what was both the purpose and the expectation for us in experiencing the thing. In adult life, there is not usually a learning menu, but more of a demand. *I need this by Tuesday…* or … *There's a leak and the basement is flooded.* (with the implication of – fix it now!) The societally expected default is that of security. Instead of throwing our arms up in ambiguous helplessness, we fain secure in our knowledge. It is likely to make someone uneasy to think that responsible adults didn't know what they were doing. Either you do the thing by Tuesday or you know how to fix the sump pump or you know how to look up the correct tradesperson to fix it – and they are just a phone call away. Confident. Secure. Solutions. All built on a bank of already-there knowledge. That's great, but it's not learning. Learning is the figuring out what you don't yet know; it is about the new and definitely includes those moments of uncertainty. When approaching something genuinely new we need to ask for explanations, seek information, find out what makes it tick, ask how it works, observe. All these are, to lesser or greater degrees, encouraged in a school environment, and rekindling that thirst at all stages in life beyond formal education is going to help us build – whatever you can imagine.

Teaching yourself

When we move away from the expectation that learning happens when we are told to do something by someone else, we are left with ourselves as teachers. This liberation can leave us feeling lost. Although it was never on a test, being able to teach yourself is one of the most valuable skills we can develop. It is useful to be taught by others, but it is not the only way, and a pure reliance on others means we are limited in how and when we can move forward, sideways, or move in any direction.

Teaching is a responsibility. Those teachers we had at school, in university, in classes at the community college, they all got paid to teach us and their salary was for a job that included preparation and planning. They were there to make sure a curriculum was laid out for us and to ensure we had a good chance of understanding through some sort of structured introduction of resources, activities, and assessment. Teaching ourselves means we are in charge. What does that mean? I could say we each have to go and make the metaphorical structure that represents teaching, where the outcome is our learning, and that might feel overwhelming, like being given a palate of bricks to drag around until finding the right place and then one by one stacking bricks until we figure out how to build a house. That sounds a gruelling, lonely, and slightly impossible pursuit, but being your own teacher does not have to be either a burden or a solitary task. Think of it more like being a construction site manager who plans, oversees, and is prepared to step in during the building process if there is a hitch. Teaching and learning take work, but you certainly do not have to carry all the weight yourself or do things the hard way. Teaching yourself should not need to be a complete reinvention of everything from scratch. You may want to build a house, but there is no reason you cannot take the bus or drive to your construction site and have the timber or bricks delivered; you can even borrow power tools or call on others to support you and help make the building process more efficient.

Teaching yourself is about being receptive, making connections, actually going through the paces of doing it, and taking the time and care to realize what you have learned. The sources and resources available to us are widespread. Traditionally for 'how to' one would get a book. The washing machine comes with a manual, so I suppose if I want to learn to knit, there's a book for that too. Yes, there is, but a book might not be the most effective approach, and certainly is not the only way to teach yourself. Some things are easier to show than write. If you say an unexpectedly nice thing to me, and I look up and give half a smile, you can *see* that, there is no need to read a booklet with a section labelled '1.1.2 Appreciation and gratitude in friendship' to learn the meaning of my smile.

Learning, expression, and understanding incorporate all our senses; we experience and recognize learning. It does not only happen through formal sources like books. One of the easiest ways to begin teaching yourself is through observation. In recent years and specifically in 2020 there has been an exponential explosion of homemade how-to videos on the internet. Finding specific resources like tutorial videos can give tailored guided bite-sized chunks of instruction. These are perhaps the easiest to spot as 'learning tools' as they come with labels like 'play the ukulele in 10 easy steps'. Remember you can learn from less dedicated sources as well and this comes in the form of recognising the unofficial teachers in settings across daily life.

The way you teach yourself and learn from others will not always be the same. By that I mean you are not going to discover a single formula that equals great learning, however consistency and meticulous noticing will contribute to the quality of your learning. A yoga teacher of mine put it simply saying, *you have to keep rolling out that mat, every day*. He was not wrong. Attention to the details of process, what works when, and how progress and results unfold will greatly contribute to your accumulating a repertoire of useful strategies.

The permutations and combinations of what you do and when you learn in one situation can inform the way you view possibilities in a new situation in the future. Your approach to learning does not have to be the same each time you take on a new task, or each time you take on the same task. There will be times when efficiency is a priority and the goal is to get directly from A to Z as quickly as possible, and other times it might be more beneficial to go slowly when new skills need to be carefully developed and shaped. This will ensure quality over speed. The exact path you take depends on each task, your goals, and a clear understanding the physical and mental requirements involved in achieving these. Instead of going from A to Z, by taking the '1, 2, skip a few, 99, 100' approach and bypassing most of the letters in the middle, you could take a slow-paced tour through a section in the latter half of the alphabet, by really focusing on the aspects of learning represented by q, r, s, and t. You might go over these letters several times, forwards and backwards, before progressing through the rest of the letters to finally arriving at Z. Different ways are ok.

As you consciously teach yourself, you will develop more of an awareness and become more likely to make informed choices, simply because these choices matter, as you are the one responsible. There is no shifting the blame to someone standing in front of the class. By taking note of the components of learning: the relationships between people (your everyday teachers) and what they can offer, the experience you can gain in different situations, the qualities inherent in different environments, and how all these work together with your efforts to impact your learning, you are in a better position to begin to synthesize a sort of curriculum, outline your learning, and make progress. Going through

these paces of noticing every step are the building blocks of
how you learn to teach yourself.

The 'coping' aspect of learning

Learning, taking in new things, actually understanding and comprehending – the whole process takes time and lots of individual steps before we get to the outcome. Those iterations of moving forward, seeming to stumble, or unexpectedly running with great strides, can click into place when we think and recognize our processes, whether through watching or doing. This active thinking part of the process is invaluable. In formal teaching settings, the teacher externalizes this for us. They reiterate, literally do or say it again for us so we can notice more easily. Then when we recreate what we have been shown, there is a greater sense of awareness and more meaning. When learning for ourselves, we take on the roles of the teacher and student as explainer, challenger, tester, thinker, and doer as we actively work through the task.

This conscious awareness takes effort. Noticing the intricacies of each progressive action and thinking these through allows progress both at the time and later. The concept of coping is to do with recognising, as opposed to simply seeing a finished product. For example, when walking by a shop window, you may see a beautiful watch, ticking, the second hand moving with precision, and might even catch a glimpse of the cogs moving back and forth. All these observations give you information about the watch. You can see the thing, in a finished state, with everything in place. There is so much you cannot gather from only seeing that kind of completed masterpiece, like the process by which it came to be and the skills needed. The *how* is simply not available, and although there are some things that can be figured out, the more specialized the product, object, or task is, there will be more levels of understanding needed to duplicate the process and learn it for yourself. I once watched a craftsman repair a Rolex, and honestly, I had no clue there even could be so much involved in something that on the surface goes 'tick'. That is an oversimplification, rather like saying I didn't realize mountain climbing was hard, but the idea holds true and we often do not realize what goes into something, nor do we realize what goes into learning and teaching ourselves. This can be applied to any discipline – culinary skills, writing, music, medicine, mechanics, art, maintenance systems – everything has deeper processes that we do not necessarily see.

Once we commit to learning, it is in our best interests to navigate those intricate details as efficiently as possible, and this is done through what is called 'coping' with the situation. Simply, it implies that all the processes become transparent and integrated into the foreground. It is not as if the teacher presents out loud, then you consider in the quiet of your mind, practice the new skill, and the only time you reveal the skill is when it is somehow fully mastered. Coping is about going through all the trials and really articulating each step with conscious awareness.

Back to the shop window example. This time instead of a watch, let's make it simple with a practical example: imagine a cake. Going from seeing the cake to baking the cake is something we might be able to begin to imagine and actually we could believe that yes, we could have a go at making a cake. Neither you nor I might be professional chefs, but chances are that we could make something edible that resembled a cake with a few steps of considered preparation. Coping means we articulate, evaluate, and realize progress as we go through our learning. What steps are there?

- I see the cake. I *observe*.
- I need to figure out what the cake is made of. This can be done through various methods of *investigation*.
- I could ask someone about the cake. I could take a knife and cut into it to see what the inside of the cake looks like. I could taste the cake, feel the cake, smell the cake. I *explore* the situation.
- I can *seek* further information.
- Going to the store, I can buy ingredients so I can *attempt* to make the cake myself.

At each stage, I choose what I do, question how it is going and whether this was a productive decision, and I evaluate.

This is by no means a comprehensive list, but it gives you an idea of some of the thinking and analytical processes that could occur as you go. There may be reflection through thoughts, self-talk, reflection on physical sensations, or by using external props or other people to help you assess how you are progressing.

The reflective element of noticing is essential when actively 'coping' with a task. Without noticing we risk taking a narrow view, and perhaps unknowingly welcoming (self) imposed limitations. The whole idea of learning involves going beyond where you are now through some form of growth. This takes agency. Without stepping out, we only know what is here. To go beyond requires vision and forethought where perhaps we meet uncertainty as we put things together, physically and mentally, manipulate them in our minds, wonder, and sometimes even guess (and that's ok) by using aspects of what we know to help us make that leap to new learning.

Self-regulation

Once we become used to recognising how we learn, there can be a renegotiation of process. We choose and regulate the ways in which we learn and do things. Really understanding the awareness of choice and knowing what an impact our active decision making really has, gives us a reason to develop an inventory of strategies and processes. These can then be combined with our ongoing knowledge of our strengths and weaknesses to allow the most informed decisions as we move forward. By building and using this base of strategies we become responsible for directing, for self-regulating our growth.

Much of self-regulation has to do with the inner-processes of thinking, the meta-thinking, the metacognition. Instead of simply buying the cake, we have all those steps and the consideration that goes alongside. In our cake list above, the actions were highlighted. As well as these active steps, there is the internal, metacognitive processing where we organise and analyse the things we do. Some aspects of this are easier to do than others. For example, as we make decisions, we can name and categorize different influences as they emerge. Paying attention to what is behind our why can help us to attribute reasons appropriately. This all is part of painting as complete a picture as possible of more than just the task as an isolated operation. No pursuit happens in a cultural or physical void, and even if you could specify the setting, **you** are unique. The way I react to something may be totally different to you, despite everything else about the task.

Our individual uniqueness makes it all the more important to learn how to think about our thinking, but being so close to ourselves also poses challenges. We are invested in what we do; we care; and we are naturally biased. Genuinely assessing our capabilities, knowing what we can do or what we might need help with, spotting what will be a struggle, stretching us and what is really quite easy requires both understanding what's going on and that we take a step back. If we are too close it is easy to get wrapped up in emotion and not look objectively. Part of the role of an external teacher is to be able to call out the times when we maybe need to do a bit more before moving ahead, and for us - without that external teacher - that means we assume that role as the self-regulator of our learning. Taking that responsibility can feel heavy, but also it can be freeing. With a teacher we have the luxury of relying on their advice – they tell us what to think, and in good cases this acts as a guide and stimulus for our own thinking, but it can be a way of offloading the responsibility we should have to our *self-* in terms of self-regulation. When we assess our own capabilities we are released from using other's judgements to qualify our thinking. Instead we make up our own minds, and then use external sources as confirmation to support our thinking instead of using others as the basis for forming our beliefs.

Keeping a mental checklist can help to keep you on track as you develop these self-regulatory skills:

- **First is to notice everything** from your surroundings to your physical and mental state. What is involved? Where do you need to go or be? What physical objects do you need? What is demanded of yourself?
- **Question**. Why is the setting appropriate? What needs to change? What is your instinct? What do you not know how to do already?
- **Name** the skills you need to learn. Make lists of the tasks you need to do, the steps you will take as you progress. What are the processes?

- **Categorize** the different tasks and things. Are they thinking things, doing things, associated, circumstantial tasks that will help you to learn? When do they happen? Categories of *type* as well as listing by *when* can help clarify what needs to be done.
- **Attribute (where appropriate)**. Why? For whom? Because of what? Knowing why as well as what impact the actions or thoughts will have is important.
- **Choose**. You are in charge and it is up to you to decide what you actually do.
- **Observe as you process and do**. When you take the step to act, keep alert and pay attention to the details. Observe the internal processes as well as the way you interact with the environment around you.
- **Be Patient**. Doing anything that involves actual learning, as opposed to simply repeating something you already know, takes time and many small and large repetitions.
- **Repeat**. These repetitions are the steps as you learn to climb. One foot at a time as you go, unless you are wearing a jet pack of course.
- **As you move, be aware**. If steps in learning are like steps in walking, sometimes there is uneven ground with dips or obstacles. Keeping your senses peeled will serve you well.
- **Analyse**. Noticing is step one, the second part of that is to clock what it means. This step is really a repeat of the above: question, name, categorize, attribute… in simple terms think as you go.

Remember to separate the skill from your self. Keeping an objective view will help you to be accurate in your thoughts, especially as you dive into the intricacies of metacognition.

- **Assess, Evaluate, and Appraise**. This is where you really begin to decide on how your progress is going. To do this effectively you need criteria. What are your judgement benchmarks? What are you aiming for? How close to the mark have you come? Know these and you can make accurate appraisals.

- **Realize**. Once a judgement is made, take it in. Internalize it and get to grips with what it means for you. Are you not quite there yet? Have you done brilliantly? (Remember not to let that go to your head. Separate the self from the judgement of achievement.)

- **Balance options**. Does it mean backtracking to do more work? Or can you take a breather because you are ahead of schedule? Maybe a breather is not the best option even if you are ahead of schedule? Weigh these up and think about them.

- **Plan the path forward**. It is important to think ahead. Planning involves vision. Think. Project. Imagine. See yourself doing it *before* you actually jump in.

- **Be aware of influences**. As you do move forward, the setting is bound to change. You are not in the same place as where you began. Realign your thinking and see if you have new influences. Are you still interacting in the same way as before? This will help you to be aware of your options.

- **Dare to step forward, with awareness**. Remember there is a false security in stillness. We feel safe when there is not change, but the world moves on. It takes a risk to move forward, and this can feel uncertain. The best chance of success comes with a secure sense of awareness of the situation and of your self. If you know you know, then you can believe. Self-efficacy leads to agency.

- **Keep questioning, paying attention, and**

evaluating. The cycle continues, and as it does, you need to keep on your toes. If you continue with the rigour and assessment then you will *know* that you are making progress toward your goal.

Throughout all of this, be willing to learn, and importantly, be willing to accept both risk and failure.

Coping with failure

Nobody likes the sound of the word failure, and even worse is to be called a failure. The red stamp of fail is often taken to mean 'inadequate' and feels final. Is it? It is a judgement of where you are at one point in time, usually against criteria. However, could we be seen to fail at all sorts of things? If failure is not doing something, then could we say that we have failed to do all the careers not pursued? Have I failed to join the army or failed to become an electrician? Did I fail to grow to six feet tall? That sounds ridiculous. There is some aspect of conscious, controlled effort associated with failure.

Some people rename failure as 'working towards'. This does negate the idea of failure as being final, but it also gives a false sense of open-ended possibility. A criterial judgement of failure is made in the now and involves the assessment and recognition of the attempt of a task. Perhaps where you are now is indeed inadequate as compared to criteria for the final goal. Is 'not yet' a good solution? It gives a positive spin on not having achieved something, but in some situations there is actually a finite window of opportunity to do a specific thing in a specific way. I miss a flight, it can feel like my plans are ruined because I will not travel to my destination as planned, but there are other ways and means. I could take a train or drive, or fly tomorrow. Will I miss an event? Maybe, and both the end product and the path to get there may look different than initially imagined, but it does not mean all is lost. Nor does it mean I, personally, am the failure. If I fail at a task, that failure is graded against specific skill and criteria-based action, and is in no way a complete representation of my person.

Where I am, or you are, is somewhere on the journey of learning and life. Knowing both where I am now and where I aim to go, and seeing the difference between those does not imply a failure to get there. Understanding that 'in progress' is not final, and so even when it is clear more ground needs to be covered, because the effort continues, you are not done can be a challenge. However the willingness to continue is what frees someone from the permanence of fail.

Realising this in the moment can be a challenge. I missed it only this morning. I often wake up early with the birds. Sometimes I walk across to the field opposite my house and watch and listen while the sun rises. This became a bit of a morning routine and I wake without an alarm, just to the faint call of the birds. On a particular morning in mid-May (this very morning) I got up and peeked through the curtain at 4:49 a.m. to see the most amazing pink mottled sky. In that moment it was unclear whether this pink was coming or going, so I dressed quickly and headed out the door in an effort to catch it on film. By the time I crossed the road and climbed into the field (which is slightly raised from the road) the fuchsia had mostly faded to a dull grey. Through my camera it looked like nothing: I failed to capture it. I was not turning back the sun or the clouds and so I turned my back and headed home, but then I thought that I may as well have a little walk as I was outside. I walked down the street and into the village, and for some reason I turned around to look the other way, and what did I see? The sky lit up again. This time there was no pink, but there was gold and it was happening while my back was turned.

It makes for a very good little parable *you never know what is happening until you look*, and the thing was that I had decided that I was looking for pink, when there were other things to see. I had 'failed' to capture the pink, but I hardly failed and there were other ways to capture the crepuscular light.

We all experience the disappointment of not achieving something. Are you going to fall down? Yes. Uncertainty – falling – is part of the learning process, but different to failing, when you fall you will get back up. Using the checks of self-regulation as you acquire new skills, and supporting your progress with positive and well-founded self-efficacy beliefs will help you to understand and deal with setbacks when they happen in the learning process.

What we do is important and so is saying no. Having the insight to choose not to do something can be the difference between succeeding to carry something or spinning one too many plate. Like vision, both metaphorical and the sight of our eyes, we need to filter and decide what the prominent things are that we want, need, and are willing to do.

Now

When we do, and there are no inhibitory or contradictory thoughts in the mind, that is when the yes overrides the no. The thinker William James called this the 'express fiat'. In Latin 'fiat' expresses a sense of 'let it be done' implying purposefully instigating something. It does not come with a sense of overcoming or grit, but of flow. Learning, doing, having agency can work in harmony with one another.

Harmony does not mean utter simplicity or sparseness. Mahler wrote swathes of rich beautiful harmonies that had complex sonorities, mixing instruments to create just the right hue of sound, and not just one note. His harmonies were chords with five or ten notes, spanning a huge range – and not all obviously fitting together, until you understood what he was after and how that fit. A harmony is a relationship; a single note is not a harmony. There is always a context to make something harmonious or dissonant, and one person's harmony is another person's dissonance.

As your now unfolds, you need to keep reorienting yourself to see where you are on the path of learning and doing, take stock of the processes of personal agency you have and what you think of these. What are your self-efficacy beliefs? Are you in a position to say yes? Do you actively question? Yes is an answer, not an assumption or a state of permanence. When it becomes *the* answer, then you have entered your now.

When the world shakes

There are some changes in the world and in life that are genuinely unprecedented across our spectrum of experience from the natural disaster of fire or disease, to less sinister things like moving house or starting a new job, and joyful things like getting married or starting a family. These all break the patterns we know and through need we learn and adapt rapidly. When the infrastructure is shaken, people are put in a position to rethink. Over the past 50 years for many people it has been possible to escape large scale negative events, and with some life changes, they are choices that we not only see coming, but choose, and this makes the transition less shocking. When we are invested in something we are more likely to commit and actively seek a positive way through, and also we take these major life events on when we are ready.

The children living through the 2020 pandemic *will* have a different perspective because of the imposed change they were plunged into and what they have witnessed, – more than witnessed, experienced. They have lived their own reactions as well as been pawns in the problem solving processes of their parents and teachers. We can learn, just as observing what is around us all the time, from the explorations of young and old as their environmental fabric unravelled. Children used (and exploited) technology. Adults tried to establish control. What resulted was newness.

As an adult there is a choice to be stubborn and say what you like, to disagree and decide not to do whatever has been suggested, but for the youth? They were dragged through the good and bad solutions. There were wonderful moments of creativity and resourcefulness as people repackaged and repurposed their time, space, and the tools – tech or otherwise – available to them. Online programmes were used for new purposes as people discovered how to connect with each other when physical contact was removed. Expected use and rules went out the window as people sought solutions. The very think tank that integrates development and operation of software (DevOps) got creative in how they circumvented the limits of not having physical collaborations and managed the risks faced by holes in security with standard online video conferencing tools, while still having a publicly accessible conference. The DevOps international conference was held inside a video game: Animal Crossing (see end note 5 for link). Keynotes, presenters, and delegates entered the virtual conference, held within the actual game via a personalized invitation link. It was livestreamed with all the trimmings of a live conference like speakers with full video presentations.There were also examples of far less effective solutions by those who were not perhaps active blue-sky thinkers. School teachers dumping pages of text and PowerPoint at children, forcing them to sit behind silent screens for hours a day. Online was adopted as a quick solution to the social isolation guidelines, and people missed a trick when they thought content equalled experience or that content equalled learning.

Out of the fire of the pandemic all sorts of new growth has, or can, come. School children experienced an unexpected opportunity for their own creative thinking, as they outsmarted the tech of student surveillance with clever backgrounds of themselves. Some learned to use their hands to sew or cook or cut their own hair. When change happens in the world at large, the change caused by something new, a 'disruptive technology', takes both vision and time to take hold within a culture. This shift, however, was imposed and happened without that period of social testing, which meant the good and bad existed. Those who lived and worked through that time experienced what both successful and unsuccessful adaptation look like. In a genuinely novel situation without prior examples to draw upon, without formal articulation or published rules about expectations, and when immersed in the unknown, successful adaptation can take us by surprise. Sometimes what works does not look anything like we imagine it should or even could be. Look at the birds; they are living, tiny dinosaurs. I doubt T-Rex dreamed the idea that becoming a chicken would be the way to survive an apocalypse.

Jumping into learning

That need to figure out learning, experience, and life is not always imposed so dramatically. Usually people plan major changes in life. We need to be in the practice of asking the questions that get asked in those very unusual situations. The questions themselves are simple, but it is the reverence with which they are considered, almost respected makes the difference.

What is happening? Why? How? And importantly what am I going to do about it?

Learning to ask these questions for yourself and not to wait for someone or something to shake you can help you to feel prepared to move – to jump into learning.

CHAPTER SIX
Words and Impacts

As heard on the playground: *'Sticks and stones may break my bones, but words will never hurt me…'*

Sometimes in life we have goals, pursuits, hobbies that somehow are dropped or suddenly cut short for one reason or another. Things, people, happenings, and the most ephemeral and insignificant seeming things can derail us completely. The whole idea behind lived self-efficacy is that we grow to believe in ourselves, our capabilities, and this leads us toward positive outcomes and achievements. However, despite achieving real success, our self-efficacy beliefs are not impervious to change, and we sometimes allow ourselves to be knocked down. The knocks can leave lasting marks and healing these marks, exorcising these demons, however you look at it, standing back up on your own two feet can be very tricky indeed.

The story of Dorothy and her song

There was a fairly ordinary girl who was not particularly tall, not particularly sporty, not in the popular crowd; she ate peanut butter sandwiches and was an eager learner with an open, curious disposition. In her last year in middle school, aged 14, she was cast as Dorothy in the school play 'The Wizard of Oz'. She duly learned her lines, sang her songs, wore the checked dress, and even had braids in her hair. The show went well; the audience applauded, and success was achieved. In terms of what we know about self-efficacy this was a classic positive mastery experience: all three performances of the play went well. There were no memory slips or missed cues, and, after each show the positive reaction of the audience reinforced the positive achievement. That girl continued to sing through into high school, taking part in the choir, but one day one of her peers turned to her in the hallway and said the sort of thing that nobody wants to hear: 'You sound rubbish. You can't sing.'

Kids say mean things to one another, but somehow those words cut deep and the girl who was once Dorothy receiving flowers on the stage to warm applause, stopped singing – just like that. She quit choir and shut her mouth. In fact those words really left a mark and she didn't open her mouth again to sing for nearly 20 years. Sure, she sang the odd chorus of happy birthday with a crowd at parties, but nothing more prominent or exposing than that. You might think her previous experience of being Dorothy with solos in front of an audience should have easily overridden a comment made by some other student at school in relation to nothing at all. But somehow it didn't, not for twenty years.

In terms of self-efficacy and the way we understand it, mastery experiences are the main things that inform our self-efficacy beliefs, and they should certainly override something someone says, some verbal or social attempt to knock them, but this time they certainly didn't. What went wrong? Understanding, creating, and maintaining self-efficacy beliefs is not so textbook in real life. Have you ever had an experience, could be something someone said, or even the way someone looked at you or reacted to something, that completely deflated you, even if for an instant? One minute confident and secure in what you are doing, and the next minute taken back, anything from a slight wobble of doubt to being ready to pack it in and quit completely? Most people have had something in life that shakes them. *That* thing that is shaken is your self-efficacy belief.

When our Dorothy did come back to singing, even two decades later, it was a rock-bottom pick-up for her, and took a couple of years of weekly one-to-one singing lessons before she gained the courage and self-belief enough to sing anything in front of anyone. That damage from that flippant comment left a real scar and the process of recovering what she had and healing wasn't at all like starting to learn with a clean slate. It was not the same road at all. It was as if before she was walking down the yellow brick road, and this time there was the odd brick, but it was mostly decay, mud, and overgrown brambles to sort through even to find a path forward. She couldn't bring herself to meet with a real singing teacher. She didn't believe in herself enough even to approach a teacher to be a 'real' student. She could only bring herself to face someone who was also a nobody. She went to someone younger than herself, less experienced, and decided it was just about ok if she was their first student – a sort of guinea pig. It was as if she didn't consider herself even worthy of learning.

That was the truth: *she* didn't consider herself even worthy of learning.

I should say *I* didn't. (It is really my story.) I was that Dorothy and *I* didn't consider myself worthy of learning and was too ashamed to approach someone who did consider themselves a teacher. A teacher has knowledge, identity, and when you learn from a teacher, you are working toward being that thing. I wasn't ready to even pretend I was on the road to learning to be a singer. Instead I learned from an undergraduate in one of my own classes. I had students who were required to teach their first lessons to someone else, just to learn how to interact and communicate with one another, as part of their undergraduate coursework in a music with teaching degree. I became the fallback student if they couldn't find someone else to teach. They could always teach me… and so my journey began. My self-beliefs were non-existent and this was a process of both learning to recognize and gain skill, as well as giving myself permission to achieve once again.

My first set of lessons was with a young man in his mid 20s, who sang semi-professionally. He was in several choirs. I was too sheepish to sing even a one-octave scale with confidence. (You know the 'Doe a Deer' song from the Sound of Music? I couldn't manage even squeaking that out.) What stuck with me was his response to me: 'But you *know* music. You teach *us*,' he said to me, looking baffled. 'I've heard you perform.' Yes, I did know music, and I could and did perform on the cello, but I didn't believe I could sing. My beliefs and confidence did not simply transfer from one to the other. Each task is different and self-efficacy beliefs are specific and highly nuanced.

I went through two student teachers over the space of several years before I gained the confidence to really learn out loud, as singing requires, and actually approach someone who already called themselves a teacher. It was two years later when I approached a woman to be my teacher. This person was different, she was still a student, but was also a very accomplished performer studying for her degree as a way to gain a formal qualification in teaching. I admired her sound greatly, that's what drew me to her, and fortunately she did not judge me as a learner but worked with me at my pace. Over the years to come, she encouraged me to allow myself to find my voice once again.

Was Albert Bandura wrong when he listed the four main influences on self-efficacy? Did he just not get how we build our beliefs? No, not at all. He definitely got the essence in his experimental studies, but what controlled experiments he historically undertook do not take into account is the complexity of life. In experimental settings psychologists can control for external influences, biases, and anything that might distort the clarity of the results they are investigating. Questions asked are specific and the settings in which they are examined are also usually quite refined. This is why experiments use what are called 'test' conditions. Jumping into real life is like moving from playing Guitar Hero to playing live at the Hollywood Bowl.

It is not an uncommon tale, where someone is dissuaded from carrying on with whatever pursuit. It could be a hobby like knitting, or swimming, or something career-focused like applying for a promotion or changing focus in your way of working. How many times have you almost proposed something but not done it for fear of what someone else might think or say? Spoken words and unspoken communications, through gesture, can be powerful, if we let them. It is important to be aware and remember that these are not inherently powerful. What happened in the story above is that Dorothy accepted the words of someone else as a replacement for her belief, without actually examining or formulating her own self-efficacy beliefs at all. She gave them the power by simply replacing what should be her own beliefs with whatever she was told. Allowing this to happen does not make logical sense at all, but people do it all the time. We hear those in authority positions often say, 'I know better' and they may well know better and have insight that we do not have, but then again they may not. What is sure is *they know differently*. They know from their perspective, and we owe it to ourselves to question, check, and make that decision about our own self-beliefs for ourselves. Without this self-checking mechanism we create a sinister situation that looks like this:

Declared Judgement (or Value) + Position of Authority (someone we trust or admire) = Blind Acceptance.

Just as there are walls and barriers to our achievement that we have explored in earlier chapters - and realized they are often not real, even though at the time they appear like mountains in our perception - there are also external influences and influencers that seem to magically take on extraordinary powers over our self-efficacy beliefs, well beyond any influence they should actually have.

Social influences

Social influences, people and what they say, should wield far less influence over our self-beliefs than our own lived experience. However, it takes a strong person not to be swayed even a little bit by the crowd. As we develop physically and mentally through childhood and adolescence, we become aware of both our inner thoughts and of the world around us. In the mix of social and personal influences in everyday life, it can be difficult to tell the sources of the voices telling us what we have done well or what is right for us. Was that something I decided or was it an idea someone else planted in my mind? Should I listen to it? Should I listen to myself? These are questions we need to ask and know how to answer. Children have an innate openness and willingness to trust. Perhaps this is partly due to the purity of not having experienced maliciousness or manipulative behaviour yet. Also, both physically and chemically the brain has yet to develop capacity to formulate the schema of consciousness that allows the complex understanding of the differences between 'me' and 'you'. For example from the perspective of a toddler, there is no difference between thinking and saying, because to their understanding we *all* express all that goes through our minds – because that is what they do. There is no sense of private thought or of a filter, or any understanding that someone might have other thoughts, positive or negative, than what they express out loud. There is not the private planning, reflecting, or considering that goes on in the adult mind, but only pure, simple communication.

As we grow older and begin school, we experience so many new situations. Children are gathered in whole classrooms filled with others their same age. It is a sort of organized social party and certainly brings engagement with others into people's lives on a whole new scale to whatever neighbourhood gatherings or care groups might have been previously experienced. There are suddenly highly organized situations instead of the early exploration of the world that happens independently and at your own pace as play or doombling around the place where you live. When they are very young, children are willing and eager to help one another learn as there is still a sense of fun, play. Building knowledge is just another form of possibility, like in a game. Unfortunately when we move from the playground to the formal setting of the classroom, rules are introduced and imposed and perspectives change.

In school children sit at desks, stand in line, answer 'here' when their names are called for the morning register, put up hands if they wish to speak. *Yes, Sally? What would you like to say?* It is so different. The teacher presents rules to follow, gives out rewards and punishments for those who step in and out of line. Soon goals are introduced through tasks - assignments, and sure enough, competition is introduced. Sometimes that competition is for attention or recognition by the teacher, and other times it is to be the best amongst peers, to win. After all, only the top 10% can go into the 'red' reading group as opposed to the less good 'yellow' group, and don't even mention the 'green' group. In school you want to be the best, beat the others. The best in school isn't generally presented as what you can do compared *to you*, but about what you can do compared to those around you or some external standard. The 'best' should be something that we determine by looking inside, at our own capabilities and how far we have gone or come, not by looking at the list of students in the class and how we can measure up compared to them. Thinking have I done as well as she has? What about him? I'm better than them, and you're no good! These fabricated social comparisons are not what self-efficacy is about.

As we grow, everything begins to change: perception, awareness, and with age comes social comparison. It takes a real awareness of process and of self to navigate the external influences that are thrown at us by the people and situations we experience.

Words: Hearing and noticing

Language is one of those magical things that lets us into one another's minds and allows us to share experience, understanding, and connect with one another. It is a wonderful mosaic of possibilities, and you know, kids say things. Adults say things too, sometimes wonderful and sometimes terrible things. Somehow I am sure that every one of us has made some flippant comment at some point in our lives, and all too often these words have to do with comparing ourselves to something or someone else, whether accomplishments, appearance, perceived value, or simply declaring that we are better. We are taught to engage with critical comparison from an early age, and it is a valuable skill. Being able to distinguish one thing from another and discerning the properties of how it works or could be used is just how we learn to make sense of the things in the world around us.

Ambiguity is common in both positive and negative communication as people do not often say what they really mean, and this makes it more difficult to understand and interpret whatever is being communicated. Consider hearing the simple warning of *'Be careful!'* which could be said with the best and most serious of intentions. It does not convey any specific context and also suffers from that missing implied object. There's no 'what' to be careful of. The problem is that people do not know what someone else is thinking, and certainly in this case there are several possibilities that could be guessed as the meaning. Depending on how well we guess the implied meaning we may or may not actually avoid the danger they are warning us about. Unless we are aware of the same context as the person saying it and share their perspective completely, we might well miss the point and take whatever was said in a completely different way than intended. Hearing 'be careful' is not enough and when filling in the blanks, people can imagine very different things: Don't talk to strangers; Wear your seatbelt; Make sure to colour in the lines; Look left! On its own *be careful* is not enough. There is so much more clarity gained by including the specific words we mean instead of leaving it to chance or someone else's imagination. Did you guess someone might have meant: *'Be careful where you step! There is broken glass on the floor.'*

When we notice a leaf floating on the breeze it does not require the same reaction as becoming aware of a baseball flying through the air toward us. Being able to make accurate judgements to understand and act upon differences as we perceive them is invaluable. People, though, are different to things; we are not as simplistic as having physical properties that mean we will follow certain rules and always behave a certain way. Our decision making is not always linear, predictable, or even rational. It is not enough to know something about some people and then to think we can have a simple comparison one person against the other and know how or what someone will say, do, or feel. Doing that disregards the complex nature of *us* and puts serious limits on what could be. I don't want anyone to limit what I can be. Don't even think it. The possibility and dream of 'can' is stifled when we engage in closed comparisons, and a learned limitation of this sort can do terrible damage to both ourselves and to others.

With a leaf or a ball, there are instant external identifiers that signal what it is and what its usefulness is to us. The thing is, people are not like that. With modern society and the things we do, the limitations of physical strength, stature, or even the ability to travel are not necessarily relevant. There may have been a time when if you were not able-bodied you could not do the only job there was as a labourer in the field, but now? Mental capacities are valued, and as the comic that first appeared in the New Yorker Magazine said: "Nobody on the internet knows you are a dog." It makes no sense to define ourselves by some external perception or mandate. We all have bodies, but that is not all we have.

Identifiers and benchmarks are useful and important for learning and goal setting, but defining ourselves by the accomplishments of others, as seen in social comparisons, recreates the very false structures around us that we should aim to free ourselves from so we can truly be in a position to say, believe, and act on the *yes I can*. It is so common to make snap judgements. When people compare themselves to others they miss the bigger picture and far more productive possibilities that arise when we compare ourselves against ourselves. People do compare themselves against others as a positive benchmarking tool, using someone else's accomplishment as a goal to strive toward, and this can be motivational. However, most often people do not take the long road but choose a faster way to promote themselves, and use words to wield power to feel stronger. *'I am the best. You are weaker.'* By means of a false or very limited comparison, it is simple for people to make themselves come out on top. It is easy to do, and creating a known structure gives the impression of feeling both safe and empowering, even if it is the exact opposite.

The power we attribute to words and those who use them can be either bad or good. The impact of words can be equally liberating as it can be damaging, and sometimes even one unexpected smile of encouragement is enough to highlight something positive that may have gone un-noticed or reinforce something we didn't quite believe without reinforcement or guidance from something or someone external to ourselves.

The people, places, and things in our lives

As we move through school and adolescence, toward whatever lies beyond – it could be more education at college or university, or a job, or some other path of caring for others, or just life, we gain understanding of the different aspects of our 'self'. Within the many settings we find ourselves, whether at home, work, or on the go, there will be a mix of different people, physical environments, real-time constraints. In our lives there is an ever-changing mix of purposeful and accidental happening, from bumping into people, being inspired to say or do something, to realising you have to go to the shop for bread. This short list precludes considering our own and others' expectations, our reasons for being there, or any goals or even plans to do anything at all. There are so many different internal and external influences at play at any one time in our lives. Life is complicated and there are seldom situations that fit into a textbook scenario. Even if something appears simple, there is still the reality that we are actually living in the midst of it, in real time, and not observing with the external gaze and level-headed mind of someone running a neat, tidy experiment. This means our decisions are not always clear, and in the heat of the moment we do our best – whatever that is.

It is a challenge to navigate and balance all the things we encounter and somehow be aware of and decide which factors are supposed to be prominent influencers, which are circumstantial or even unrelated distractions, what action is required of us, what is possible? How can we maintain a clear head allowing for accurate judgements of self-beliefs to best inform the decisions needed as we go on, living everyday. Over time and with a learned practice of awareness, we can develop a sense of personal direction, agency to shape how we fit in various situations life gives us.

If we managed all that we would all be amazing, or at least we would be in a position to formulate accurate self-efficacy judgements that could then work with our aspirations, and we would see the path forward to achievement. In the real world however, certain elements are prominent, and importance is attributed to different factors, things or people, at various times in our lives, whether they should have this authority or not. Sometimes our judgements and decisions about ourselves and our self-beliefs are sound. On other occasions, even without conscious decisions, we happen fortunately, whether by chance or design, to fall into the good hands of friends, teachers, or people who exhibit a sense of vision and seem to guide us toward becoming the best version of ourselves. And then there are times we are not so lucky. Developing our capacity for awareness and decision-making is helpful.

When we become aware of who's really in charge (ourselves), and importantly where we *believe* the control resides (with ourselves), we are in a position to understand the potential for influence in a situation (and begin to find our yes). It is easy to misattribute responsibility or to not realize what or who is influencing us, and often we do not realize that ultimately we are in charge of our actions. It is up to each of us, individually, to think through situations, questioning, assessing, and reassessing as we move through time.

Understanding perceptions

Consider the structure of a social situation similar to Dorothy's story where there is a verbal exchange between a couple of people, and one person makes some judgemental statement directed toward the other person. How is this received? Is it believed? What is the impact on the person? Above, our Dorothy simply allowed herself to accept and believe what the other person said, taking it to heart as if it was golden truth or law and allowed those words to influence the direction of her life for the next couple of decades. Putting it like that and looking at the situation objectively makes it sound absolutely nonsensical that someone would do that. How often are we prepared to automatically believe something someone else says?

Many people do believe what they hear without question. Across history, there are examples where so many people have believed simply on someone's word, it has been enough to sway the direction of entire nations on a simple slogan of lies. All it takes is an extremely confident speaker and a listener who is either willing to doubt themselves and allow the speaker to fill that doubt with their words, or a listener willing to give the speaker credibility whether they deserved it or not.

When someone says something, giving advice, making a statement, sharing their reaction through gesture or word, they essentially communicate their perception about that person, thing, or happening as they understand it at that moment in time. If someone says something about you, making a verbal judgement, this is their perceived understanding of something in relation to you at a given time. What you then do with that communication is up to you, and whether you are pierced by the pointed edge of their words or dismiss them like some yapping thing barking at the wind really can impact your whole world, from your general outlook to specific self-beliefs and how you choose, plan for, and carry out future actions.

If you, as the listener, perceive the speaker to be experienced or knowledgeable, you may decide this person appears qualified or able to speak with authority. If they can adequately judge the skills needed to carry out a task, you may choose to believe what you hear. Someone can earn or even deserve credibility and believing their reaction to or judgement of a situation or performance may be the right decision. We can also miss truths if we require people to have external signals of authority and perhaps they speak meekly and do not sound or look assertive. However, assuming someone has the authority, believing blindly, and unthinkingly granting someone power to dictate what we believe can have lasting negative impacts. Sometimes we go beyond believing the face value of words or actions and attribute a meaning that is lasting and deterministic to a statement of judgement. Dorothy not only believed a statement of 'you can't sing', but went further to interpret and accept them as saying 'you are incapable' and therefore 'you can never do this [singing]', giving childish words an enduring power over self-belief, over her understanding of ability now, and over the possibility of future capability.

People become our oppressors when we allow their words and actions to carry weight. We must be able to assess *what* is being said as well as then making sense of whether or not we choose to be influenced by it. It is up to us whether we see these would-be oppressors as some mythical warrior wielding a sword or are simply a noisy little thing yapping in the wind.

For example:

If you are uncertain about your health and seek a doctor's advice, the doctor might say, 'You are unwell. You have tonsillitis.' You will most likely believe the doctor for several reasons.

1. **Valid Qualifications:** Medical doctors undergo years of training and are considered reliable and respected professionals who are supposed to give health advice.

2. **Personal Reassurance:** You can check your throat, temperature, or other symptoms, and verify the doctor's assessment.

3. **Objectivity:** The comment is not perceived as a value judgement about 'you' as a person. Even if your head feels a bit hot and you can't swallow so well, when the doctor confirms an illness, it is not common to suddenly feel like a bad person. The doctor's assessment is not perceived as a direct threat to your 'self' and therefore should not impact your self-beliefs. In fact most people will accept a doctor's advice as a factual commentary on their physical or mental state.

Coming to the decision to accept the doctor's words as true then informs us about future steps for action. Generally after accepting a diagnosis, a next move will be to seek and take advice on how to get better. If there is a course of rehabilitation, rest, or medicine that will restore health, people commonly pursue the recommended path to healing. They will not feel less of a person or suddenly have self-doubts about their capabilities to do things because they were unwell. In fact it would be very odd if someone did decide to pack it in and quit being a writer, say, being unable to continue on that path in life because of the impact of catching a curable virus (instead of looking for a way to get better). Even suggesting that sounds farcical, but this is exactly the sort of reaction we sometimes allow ourselves to have when other people offer advice or opinions about us or our accomplishments. With a slight change in scenario, for example replacing tonsillitis with advice on how we look or sound, we can imagine how easily advice is allowed to impact our concept of 'self'.

When advice or an opinion is unexpected, unsolicited, and unwanted it is more likely to catch us off guard. If we actively seek advice, there is more of a chance that we are prepared to receive it, reflect on it, and act on it. When something out of the blue comes along, how we receive this tests the very nature of our learned habits and reactions. Is it our habit to listen, question, and reflect or do we simply hear and decide? It takes cultivated practice to assess and process what is happening around us in an objective and balanced way.

Communication

People react and say things because they perceive them, and communication in life is a series of intersecting, expressed perceptions. When we are on the receiving end it makes sense to pay attention with all our senses as communication, connection, and our own perceptions are how we learn. We need to decide *if* and *how* the things people say or do are reasonable, relevant, or perhaps even can help us.

Criticism

I was once walking with a colleague and a student. It was an informal setting, and the colleague asked a question that he often asked of his own students, about their projects. The way the student answered showed he didn't think while communicating, and wasn't aware either of his own processes or how others would hear and take his words. The colleague said to the student, *'How is your project going? Can you tell me about it?'* The student replied, *'Oh, it's good. Going great.'* He smiled, and offered nothing further. The colleague smiled too, and said, *'Well that's nice you think so. Why don't you tell me about the project and then I can make up my own mind as to how it's going.'* The student really didn't know what to do. He was shocked at such a reply and it was something he had not encountered before – the listener wanted him to give evidence so they could make a qualified decision. There were not going to be any assumptions, nobody was going to be simply taken at their word without some proof.

If a comment is not purely objective like a comment noticing *'your shirt is red'*, but instead gives an opinion or judgement about something about us or something we have done, *'you look fantastic in that red shirt'* there are any number of possible reactions we could have to interpret remarks and reactions in different lights. The reactions we have will be very different if the comments are positive as opposed to negative. Here are some caricature responses to demonstrate a range of possible reactions to the statement:

'You have underperformed.'

Initial reaction:	What is happening here?
No I didn't.	Denial
It wasn't my fault.	Attributing the result to external sources
(cry)... (sob) I'm not very good.	Accepting the comment as a definitive personal judgement
Yes, I haven't finished learning about it yet.	Partly attributing worth to the comment, but maintaining the comment to be about the 'performance' and not about your 'self'.
I did perform, and you noticed.	Not allowing immediate influence, but reinforcing that you have achieved, even if that person does not rate the accomplishment well
This is your opinion, and you chose to share it with me.	Simply acknowledging the existence of the other and actively separating it from being attributed to, or having any personal impact on you

The comment is someone else's perception. They may completely believe it to be true. The meaning we give it depends on our perspective. Every word in that sentence is important. The meaning is attributed or assumed by us. To understand how and why this happens we need to unpack everything about the comment and the situation in order to understand how we made up our own minds. Who said it? Why? What was the setting? Was the comment warranted?

How does our understanding of what was said impact us? What are the implications for what we do next? We need to question and assess everything.

Perhaps it was true that our performance was under par. Why? Let's assume that there were no external factors involved to sabotage the performance, no natural disasters came into play, and that physical environment was amenable, and any equipment involved worked. Even though the comment we received was not so nice, if the environment wasn't against us, then it may well be a fair reflection of the performance as it was delivered. Either we understood what needed to be done, but the performance was under-prepared or there was a fundamental lack of awareness of the skills necessary to successfully deliver the performance and the underperformance reflected a gap in our actual ability level at the time of delivery. Both of these are possible reasons for underperformance and both happen all the time in real life situations. Understanding the criterial nature of a task is a significant forerunner to the planning and learning that take place before we can carry out a task. Not everyone really knows what it takes to do something and the most effective way we learn is by actually doing it. Learning involves failing many times over in preparation, and even after what we think is adequate preparation, sometimes we miss the mark in the final delivery on the day.

So what if a performance does go wrong and somebody decides to let you know about it? Criticism is never particularly enjoyable to hear, and can be harder to accept. It is important to step back and remember first that it is someone else's perspective. Then question what was said, asking why do they think that, and then you can be in a better position to interpret the criticism, deciding what it means for you and what you can or should do about it. If the criticism alerts you to a skills gap, and you can identify the area to improve, and then find a way to develop and raise your skill level, that can bring you several steps toward delivering a future performance at the level you want.

This approach takes level-headed, objective, analytical thinking and helps to keep the value judgements we make about our 'self' separated from understanding the who, what, and why of process. It enables us to minimize unnecessary self-damage from the way we hear, interpret, and react to what others say and do. Just like everything we do, it takes time and practice to learn and implement this approach. Taking words and actions at face value and using the criticism and reaction of others to understand how they perceive us and our actions can help to maintain a healthy balance of self-concept, specifically our self-efficacy beliefs, and can maintain our capacity to look forward and not get stuck.

You Can't. You shouldn't. You *won't*. …or will you?

When a most severe, negative reaction is shared it might convey some aspect of someone's opinion they genuinely believe and perceive to be true, or unseemingly as it sounds, it could be planned as some act of maliciousness intended to cause mental or emotional harm. Either way, negativity can shake the best of us. It is important to examine and understand the what and why that lies behind the comments whenever we receive feedback or experience a reaction of this sort. People do sometimes act in ways simply intended to damage others. We must recognize this is not authentic critical feedback and it makes sense to dismiss it as enacted anger. This positive action of completely dismissing and not attempting to give credit to an angry rant can avoid unnecessary upset and prevent mistakenly attributing any value or meaning that could allow someone's aggressive outburst to influence our self-beliefs, future direction, or wellbeing.

Understanding negativity

Negative reactions can be valid, and even with strong (valid) negative feedback it is important to process it and question what is behind it, unpacking the words or the reaction from the task being described, to understand and move forward. It is very possible to attempt a task, have the outcome judged quite fairly as a failure, and not to have this failure result in a severe negative influence on your self-efficacy beliefs. For example, when baking a cake perhaps you confuse the temperature marking on the recipe reading Celsius as Fahrenheit and set the oven to a very incorrect low temperature. The result would be a definite failure when you produce an only half-baked cake. Watching you cut into the cake and discover it has a gloopy centre, your fellow cake-eaters might react with the judgement, *'You failed!'* This may be completely true in part, but they have communicated poorly and actually their misuse of words is much more a failure on their part.

Remember if someone says *'you failed'* to realize *there is a bit missing* from that statement. Grammatically there is an implied object that is completely absent from the sentence. They could correctly say *'you failed at* x', and in this case the *x* would be 'making a fully baked cake', but words can be blurted out unthinkingly in an instant, instead of carefully chosen. This happens especially when emotions run high.

It is easy to hear and translate *you* failed into *you are a* failure, however the implication is not that you somehow failed at being you or at being a human, but that you failed at a task. You failed *at something*. We all fail at tasks all the time and it is entirely possible to address this with strategic thinking, planning, and action. I failed to heat up my soup. I thought I heated it, but when I tasted it I found it was still cold. I decided to heat it some more. Easy. That process is called learning. Understanding how to seek and pursue a strategic approach will help avoid unnecessary influence on your self-beliefs and will help you to understand the processes involved in learning – the investment in time, and physical and mental energy needed to raise skill levels and gain experience as you work to improve your performance of that task.

Being told *'you can't do x'* can feel specific, and definitely pointed personally at you about a definite thing. It is easy to see the jump to *'I am no good'* and *'I should not do x'*, but these emotive leaps are huge and illogical. They misplace the meaning and allow for a very negative impact. There is very little chance that anybody is uniquely qualified to see into your future and declare what you can or cannot do. Only you can make that judgement about your capabilities. We have seen more impossibilities accomplished through time than learned people ever thought possible. (I chose those words carefully) Personally I think *who are you to say what I can or cannot do something?*

It does seem easier to make the leap to allow meaning to become a personal sentence with negative than with positive feedback. It goes back to that cultural training to accept the negative. Do we individually allow for the reality that each of us can be good, perhaps already is good at what we are doing. Can you honestly look in the mirror and say *'yes I can'*?

If you can do that, are you able to go one step further and say *'yes I can, and yes I am'*. That is the step that stands up to the outburst and deflates the power assumed in unfounded negativity. Optimism is a projected vision of confidence for a future reality. There is a difference between a non-descript, distant hope for the future and a belief that the better option will come into being. With self-efficacy, strategic thinking, and that vision to dream specifics, you have a far greater chance of finding a way to make those goals of your *yes* into a reality.

Praise

It is interesting to consider what happens when we receive criticism that is positive instead of negative. When someone says you have overachieved, exceeded expectations, or simply that something was great, how willing are we to receive positivity and accept praise? DO we accept positivity more easily or readily than negative feedback? There is a strong Western cultural bias toward the concept of being told 'no'. For example, in the Frequency Dictionary of Contemporary American English the word 'not' comes at 29th, with early entries being taken by words like 'a' and 'the'. 'No' follows at 86th place. It is not until entry number 263 that 'yes' makes an appearance. We are trained to be not good enough. We are assessed at how well we do, but it is often framed in terms of how much we fail. Yes we do need to be aware of shortcomings and gaps in skills, but we also need to constructively recognize and accept success.

For each person receiving praise can be a very different experience, ranging from very easy to something that is quite challenging and may seem awkward at best. It can be very difficult to even acknowledge achievement, let alone critically engage with positive reactions from others. If people are used to progress being framed in terms of counting flaws, then allowing and accepting genuine praise instead of being fed negativity can leave people not knowing what to do. Imagine an overachiever who has spent a lifetime of striving, through various activities in school and life. *Always* striving means that no matter what ground is covered, they never quite arrive, repeatedly falling short of the mark, and highlighting the negative is expected. That person is used to failing; they have trained themselves to expect to find elements of failure and then use these as reasons for continuing to push forward. They reinforce that there are still gaps in their knowledge, perpetuating a belief in inadequacy and underachievement, and believing there is always more to do before true achievement is attained. The idea of being done is an alien concept for an overachiever. Even when they do reach what would be recognized externally as an obvious accomplishment, they will still tend to diminish its worth and somehow declare there still to be aspects of failure present even if there are none. These people need to develop the skills to examine and accept praise for achievements, especially when praise is given unexpectedly.

Granting yourself permission to accept and own your achievements, whether positive or negative, is important. It can make someone feel vulnerable to allow that there can be either positive or negative reactions to them and their work. Others can see who you are and what you do through their own eyes. If we start with this unbiased approach to receiving criticism (positive or negative) then we can assess the given situation with integrity, and learn from it. Part of 'yes' is a willingness to take responsibility and own achievement, and for someone used to finding failure, accepting success can be just as much a challenge as hearing criticism may be for someone else.

Just as with negative responses or criticism, people can infer meaning about positive comments that is well beyond anything to do with their abilities, and attribute it to be about *who they are*. Sometimes praise for achievement is mistaken as praise for self. As with Dorothy, when she believed in negativity and gave it false value, it had lasting damaging consequences. The same dangers exist with believing positive comments and falsely taking these as a form of personal affirmation.

You performance was great ≠ *you* are great.

The performance may have been great and in that performance, in that moment you may have been great, but there is danger in assuming a wider transference to life, the world, and everything. A performance is a single, specific, criterial task and your overall concept of 'you', your self-image, is wider than any one thing and is not built off of one situation. Accepting praise for one specific thing as automatically relating to 'you' in general may well be filling you with false security.

Where positive judgements are concerned, there is a definite line between developing the headiness of overconfidence and maintaining a healthy acceptance and critical engagement with complimentary feedback. Lavishing in gratuitous positivity can quickly descend into a session of back scratching and purring that is neither productive nor truly meaningful, and it is certainly not beneficial to a well-founded sense of self-efficacy. Like criticism, compliments reflect a perception of what has happened, and the greater the compliment the more you may have exceeded the expectations of the person giving the compliment, but that judgement is still formed within the bounds of their perception. False and unchecked praise can limit your understanding of an achievement, like the fish who believes it 'owns' a small bowl but somehow cannot see the walls that hold him inside his cage.

A Checklist:

- Separate skill from self.
- Evaluate and appraise.
- Assess and reassess.
- Name, categorize, and process influences.
- Attribute reasons.
- Assess capabilities instead of judging by what others think.
- Be willing to learn.
- Allow the risk of accepting failure and success.

Work not to base your judgements on those of others but to

qualify and contextualize them with your own understanding. Others can witness what you do, but you know your capabilities. Even if you do not know the full extent and possibility of what can be realized through the 'yet' of your capabilities in the future, you will be the most accurate judge of how you perform. If you use all your faculties and senses, all your attention, this information can balance and check what someone else says and you will begin to form your own beliefs.

CHAPTER SEVEN
Reinforcing YOU CAN

Having looked at self-efficacy from a theoretical point of view and considered several different situational influences on our beliefs, it is time to turn attention to our perception of what is possible for us to achieve. The can in *Yes I Can* refers to capabilities, and our approach to this idea of 'can sometime in the future', and how self-efficacy can influence possible options is important. When our thinking starts with the idea of possibility, it is far easier to recognize something slightly new or different that would otherwise remain unnoticed or hidden from view. We learn to recognize accomplishments, beginning with what we already do, and look at our growing bank of skills to see how these can lead us forward as we embrace new opportunities.

The decision and judgement making process is unpicked and analysed with everyday, practical examples. How our perception, skills, capabilities, expectations, and risk are weighed and balanced in our thinking works to determine first whether or not we recognize the 'can', and then whether we move forward to act and transform the 'can' into a 'do'.

Finally, with tools and techniques we can now consider how to use them as we move forward. One of the biggest challenges is learning to look at the here and now and experience it in a productive way. Honing the skills to assess what is going on around us, both on a micro and macro level and learning to synthesize and decide what exactly we would like to focus on will help guide us toward our goals. This assessment is more complex than an arithmetic exercise as there is both the influence of the past and projected future to consider, or to deal with.

Capabilities and how we think of them

Can is the not yet decided, the could be, on the cusp of becoming. Can is unknown to others, but visible to your mind's eye. And yet it is not until we do, and carry out the 'can', that we find the reassurance or confirmation from the world that it is indeed possible. The essential part is that we need to *know*, to believe and have the sense of vision of the possibility of can in order to do it.

This is hard, especially if you have to keep something going inside or in process for a while before there is a stage where you can have any confirmation that yes, you are on the road not just to possibility, but to arrival. I sometimes take inspiration from the sun, as it rises every day and keeps going. But the other day I noticed something else, smaller and less noticed. I noticed the birds. The blackbirds rise every day before the dawn and sing their song. The rise up like daisies or clover from the ground and take to the tree tops and chimney pots to sing. They start before the sun and the song of each blackbird – whether a statement, call, or reply to claim territory or say hello - they sing *like clockwork*, and they do it with complete resolve. They do not seek approval or visibility, yet they are there and they sing, somehow they do and they rise up and the world is better for having them there. On the day when I got up before the dawn and happened to notice them, they made such an impact. What else have I not noticed? And what can I take from this experience?

I started wondering what do I do that happens every day, like clockwork that I do with complete resolve? The things, the habits, they are imbued with skills. Take the most ordinary of simple things – how to navigate the route to work or the coffee shop or to your child's school or the store. What do you do? Wherever you go and whether you walk, cycle, or drive you are exhibiting and putting into practice not only the common memory of the map required to get there, but daily, there is a world to navigate. You may not even realize it. If your image is of getting that pre-work morning coffee, you may well be feeling sub-par until that kicks in, but still the road to the coffee is an active *I can*.

It is imperative to understand the very real possibility of an incredibly negative impact that can result from not noticing, not finding the can, and not acting upon it.

'How capable are you?' is a question like looking into the sky and asking about the clouds. What do you see in the clouds? (have a look and notice what you think) First there might be nothing, hardly distinguishing one blob or wisp from another but using our perception and knowing how to look can soon make the nothings come into focus as somethings, with texture and their own qualities: fast, slow, changing, feathery, solid, and stormy. Clouds might remind us of something else or we might think of what they can become or do, whether they might bring rain or wind or shade. Being capable is about the potential, the possibility of what you or I could do. That cloud could rain (and it could rain on me!) but it hasn't happened yet. The idea of can is about something in the future.

The *'can'* is in there, we just have to see it.

When we say *'I can'* it doesn't always mean the same thing to everyone. Right now, think of some thing to do, hold that task in your head and say about it: *'I can do …(whatever it is)'.*

Now is that something you have already done? When you said you *'can do it'* did you mean you have the ability to do it right now? Is it something you hope to do and you are sure you will be able to do it – something you believe you can do in the future? Or is it something you believe you will do but there is considerable distance to cover before you can do it? Remember that knowing you can do something comes from seeing results. Test give results; tests measure ability. Tests show that snapshot of demonstrated skills and *can* is slightly different. It is not did or do, but includes the hope of what could be instead of stating the has been. There is not a test for capability – for the can. You determine that.

The concept of capabilities, as a belief that you can do (something) in an uncertain future, is the active pursuit of yes. In order to have an understanding of capability – even if the context can be predicted or presumed as stable, it is never known for sure, but still to understand and say you are capable, there must be an underlying belief in yourself and about your self-efficacy for that task. There is an element of active thinking that goes with developing an understanding and awareness of capabilities. It is not just something to consider when prompted, but often, and even always. Think about things, activities, tasks, and ask yourself: *How can I do this?* Actively thinking around, dreaming of, and imagining yourself as if projected into the space are all steps to take in finding the capabilities you ~~have~~ *could develop*.

At the time of writing, in 2020 there were incidents across America and the UK where people noticed some things for the first time in years. They noticed the treatment of people. They noticed the statues and what they represent. They not only noticed, but they found their can and came together to do. In years gone by thousands, and even millions of people have passed through the streets of cities and walked right by statues glorifying slave owners portrayed as gallant men elegantly dressed, looking into the sky, perhaps on a horse or with a sword or rifle. I'm sure you have seen statues in the park and walked right past them.

There is a difference between peripherally seeing a thing in the landscape and noticing, in your mind with thinking and feeling, noticing what something is, how it impacts you, and what it means to have it there. After the brutal killing of George Floyd, an innocent black man, people across walks of life *noticed* in the true sense of the word. They noticed that someone else's 'can' had been made manifest, allowing actions to be condoned, proceed and develop unchecked, and to continue down a that path for so long that whole societies had been built around principles that were unbalanced and in no way just. People didn't notice, or maybe saw and didn't really notice for a very long time, and it took being jolted into reality by the horror of the public execution of George Floyd, to make them see, and still only some saw.

Let's not allow our own lives to take that much to let us notice what's around us. Let's notice our can while we can stop and take a deep breath. Even on the most cloudy, storm ridden mornings, the sun is still there. The sky still lightens, even if we cannot see it directly. Sometimes it is from the circumstantial cues that we can recognize and realize our own stability.

Sometimes reinforcing the yes has to do with the self-noticing. And then there is the getting on the rooftop, the telephone pole or fencepost and singing your song, because we do exist in the world and that context is important.

Everybody uses the word *can*, but for some people it is about stating, almost confirming their ability and for others it is about a possibility that exists but has not been realized. When we engage and do claim our capability, we can positively reinforce both the skills and realize the capabilities we have.

CAN as possible

CAN = capabilities

Can is not **did**.
Can is not **have**.
Can is *possible*.

The challenge in *can* is in learning to see the possible, and this means new thinking. It takes effort and there is some considerable distance from seeing and doing the possible. It happens when we are removed, paused from the flow of the normal and we take that moment to think. It can be on purpose or we can be somehow boxed in and in a position where there seems nothing else to do but think around where we are.

Being boxed in can either be benign or forced.

As a small child, aged 6 or 7, my mother punished me for some act of defiance, and I was grounded which meant being shut in my bedroom with no toys or books, no games or tv for the day. I didn't cry. I wasn't sad. I looked at the situation and decided that if I did something unexpected it would give me the upper hand and show that what she intended as a punishment became a bay for productivity. I cleaned the room, not just picking up socks and making the bed, but I picked up every bit of lint from the rug and cleared all the dust off every surface there was. I had a lovely day and when she came back, her wrath was completely wasted on me. It was not a punishment and I was never grounded again.

In daily life there are awkward situations where we have the opportunity to think wider. When you run out of ingredients and can't get more for whatever reason, what do you do and why? How can the things you have, whether physical or skills, be used to do or make something different?

This comes about in everyday life when there is an intersection between *can* and *need* that leads to the potential to *do*. The problem with actual need is it gives people desperation and sometimes the choices made are not ideal or even sound. Thinking under pressure was explained to me extremely effectively in a performance class at university. It was a performance class where students got up and performed whatever music they were working on in front of their classmates and a professor, who would then make public comments about what they heard. Every week it was a different professor and on this particular week it was not a cellist and I don't think I anticipated that particular class would be overly memorable for me, but it was. What I heard was a story about learning and the decisions we make that related to performing, but also to life.

Imagine you are standing in front of a field of corn and it is tall and you have the task of getting to the other side, but you can't see anything but the corn right in front of you. You have to start somewhere so you start using your arms and legs to move and bend the corn. As you walk you make a path and leave tracks; this is like learning, practising a new piece of music. Sometimes you do it right and other times you make mistakes, but no matter where you go you are leaving tracks in the field, and you are also leaving tracks in your mind. Eventually you do get to the other side and now you know the way – you can see it clearly looking at where you've gone, but now we come to the performance and there are different constraints. You start at the same place, standing in front of the field, but this time there are people on horses with dogs behind you and when the starting gun fires, you run. You run fast and your brain will take you down the biggest path it sees in front of you. *If you have practiced incorrectly and made lots of wrong turns, and the 'wrong' path is bigger than the correct path, your mind will take you there,* and you will be in trouble.

This corn field story was a vivid picture of what happens when a musician is on stage in front of an audience, with all the adrenaline of live performance, but also in so many situations in life. We need to practice making those decisions, creating the path we want to go down so that when we are put in a truly awkward situation we are prepared and primed to think and act in a way that helps us. Nobody wants to wait until they run out of food or can't pay rent to figure out how to make ends meet. We have to learn to practice that kind of thinking, of the possible, before we find ourselves in truly severe situations that demand change, as then it is often too late to mitigate what has happened. It is far better to be the one in the driving seat.

Instead of waiting for there to be *can* and *need,* we can learn instead to instigate the change before those unexpected, and unwanted, moments happen. We can find and create within us a setting where there is *can* and *want* and this can act in the same way. The difference is the 'want' situation is under our control instead of something imposed on us. In a simplistic way, *want* manifests itself an internal *need,* in the sense of a driving force that is very much tangible and could be realised or immediate, as opposed to the never-never of saying 'I want that', and meaning 'would like' or 'wish for'.

Rehearsing possibilities is more than blue sky thinking as a dream or combination of optimism and hope. There are people who focus on the hope, such as in these affirming words of the Dalai Lama in June 2020:

Dalai Lama ✅
@DalaiLama

All human beings have the capacity to be determined and to direct that determination in whatever direction they like. Realizing we have this potential gives us a fundamental strength, enabling us to deal with any difficulty, whatever situation we are facing, without losing hope.

10:30am · 30 Jun 2020 · Twitter Web App

There will always be an element of optimistic projection in imagining possibilities, as nobody wants to fail, however understanding your *can* and realising capability are also grounded in skills and engaging with strategic planning, and they do require us to embrace real uncertainty. It is a not simple light switch of going from nothing to yes, I can. If it were that simple, nobody would hesitate to take on new tasks.

Newness

The real challenge of possibility is when it is new. New is unknown. New is scary. New is all uncertain. Even if we think they are, things are rarely actually entirely new to us. The way we perceive things around us is not necessarily balanced. Here is a simple practical example: Have you ever taken a picture of the rising moon because it looked big and you wanted to capture that, but the picture shows a small white dot? Maybe you wanted to take a picture of a boat or a car on the road in the context of a landscape and a similar thing happens. If you haven't done this before, give it a go. I have countless pictures of the moon and I am absolutely sure it was bigger. At least it looked bigger to me, but somehow in the unbiased lens of the camera, it was subsumed, brought in as part of the whole and its actual proportional place in the picture gets reflected.

The same principle holds true for many things we do. They are big to us, looming, and made up of completely foreign actions or feelings. Understanding what is necessary to approach a task, and making the connection that we already use related skills or underlying processes involved in that new task in some other familiar context can suddenly allow us to realise that this seemingly 'new' thing is perhaps not entirely new after all. It has to do with the connection between micro and macro. Here's an example well within your grasp, in fact it starts with your clasp of your hand.

Look at your fingers and the different joints going from your shoulder down to your fingers wrapped around this book, whether holding a paper copy or reading on a tablet, phone, or computer. There are two knuckles in each of our fingers, and they can only move in certain ways: they can either bend or straighten (flexion and extension). It is important to understand that range of motion, both to know what is available to us and to understand the mechanics of how this can be applied practically to various situations. At the point where the fingers connect to the hand there is another joint, and this brings a different range of motion. Now the whole finger can move side to side, forward and backwards, and around (flexion, extension, abduction, adduction, circumduction). At each place in the arm as we move from our fingers to our shoulders there are specific ways of moving, as allowed by each type of joint. As we add the knowledge and possibilities of the joints, what results is a complex array of possibilities for how we can move with elegance and precision. The nuance that allows the ballerina to throw and catch his partner or balance her on his hands all come from building and training a series of simple, understandable options that stem from motions that can be individually executed by everyone with working arms.

Although there is nothing scary or complicated in understanding the concept of how to bend a finger or an elbow, and we can readily test it out, it still does not either mean that we can see the connection between that and the end goal or stop us feeling a new situation is daunting or even impossible. If someone asked me to balance another person overhead on my hands I would definitely say 'nope, no way'. That does not mean it is not possible, just that I shut the door before attempting to discover anything about the journey that might be involved to go from here to there.

Even if we cannot initially see it, most new tasks and situations do build from a series individual simple decisions, motions, or skills and then they increasingly develop. Situations can be unnecessarily complicated by our biased perception. Use my fingers and hand to write, sure, but ask me to paint – oh, I could never do that?! They use the same parts of the body, use the ideas of converting abstraction to visual representation on paper, and use fine manual motor skills. Even though the outcome is different, there are similarities. Perception and personal bias are funny and not the same for any of us. A small insect to you is a monster to me and that beautiful resonant sound that I hear can be your terrifying thunder. It is neither possible to separate the human aspect from our experiences, nor would it be desirable to sterilise our experiences. We can notice and work to put our biased perceptions into a healthy perspective that allows us to still approach and embrace new possibilities.

When we begin by looking at the intersection of what is needed to accomplish the task and at our own existing bank of skills it can be possible to see how these can lead us forward as we embrace new opportunities. There is a balance to strike between all the different factors involved in seeing and then believing in new possibilities. The conscious awareness we have of concrete, factual knowledge, includes understanding the steps, processes, learning, and progressive achievements that will help along the way to the goal. There will also be the aspects that are unknown, either because they are unseen or potentially there is a genuine ignorance of what is required or how much personal investment of time or effort it will take to get to the new goal. Our emotional and perceptual biases certainly affect our view of how realistic a possibility is. These biases might already be known to us as worries or fears, or could surface unexpectedly, or exist without our realising they exist at all. Finally when approaching something new, we have to deal with those unexplained gut reactions that result from subconscious calculations and processes that have not yet been brought to the forefront of our understanding.

When we decide

There is a big difference between the certainty of abilities and the projection of capabilities. When those visions become commitments, those decisions are naturally linked to the practical context of the where and how, the here and now. The decision to commit and make a capability become a reality comes from you and is taken from your perspective. Knowing the answer to the question, *'where is your edge?'*, and even more, being aware of what tips you over to say *yes* (or what holds you back), is valuable. Sometimes different factors weigh heavier in that decision making process.

Every day I run two miles for various reasons: for health, for sanity, to feel my body work, and to be with myself in the outdoors. What does it take though for me to get out there and do it? This is not a new task, we are not talking about a new possibility or some capability that is yet to be realized; I know I can physically run and I have done it for hundreds of days. Some days the sun shines and the air is warm, and all the conditions are just right, and on other days the conditions are very different outdoors. On a day when the wind blows and it is spitting blobs of cold rain it is so easy to wrap up with another blanket in bed instead of getting dressed right away. The physical can is not enough, not even if I know I have a track record of good runs.

There is a tipping point where we decide any task is something to pursue instead of an idea. That decision starts with the belief in the *can*, having self-efficacy is a personal statement of belief that the possibility could become real, and then the commitment takes into account other personal factors like the effort required, the want that drives us, and the value we get from doing it. We might not know everything involved if the task is new to us, and that means we could make an incorrect decision about what is involved or how much it takes to do it. If I know I can run two miles but decide to run five, and do no extra preparation, I might find exhaustion sets in at mile four and I don't make it quite as far as I had hoped. The decision to do something does not in itself ensure success, but it does mean we put that first foot forward.

Why not? Risk.

There is one more thing that should be considered, that people think they know about but is often at best misunderstood and at worst overlooked completely: risk. Awareness of risk can keep us from entering into a task that can cause undue harm, it can make us alert so we can alter our course, or it can keep us from things as fear of the unknown yet possible consumes us.

Risk is the probability that something will occur multiplied by its impact. Some things are very likely to occur but have a very small actual impact (and that can be very different to what we perceive as the impact) and there are other things that are perhaps equally likely to occur but have a far greater impact, yet we do not seem overly concerned about them. For example, people worry about losing their wallet and having their bank card stolen, when in reality both the likelihood and the impact of this happening are pretty small. Even if someone managed to take your bank card and spend thousands on it, one phone call to the fraud team would put a freeze on the card and a few days later any money spent is likely to be refunded. The impact would be an inconvenience but not something that would genuinely affect daily life.

Something like losing a job would have a far greater impact on all aspects of life, but people tend to worry far more about losing their wallet than losing their job. Worrying about something is not really the right way to put it. People do not do anything about it *before*. Acting on these two important considerations could make such a difference:

1. Make checks to prevent whatever the risk is from happening in the first place.
2. Actively take steps to mitigate any possible negative effects of the risk's impact through pre-emptive planning and action.

What does this look like when it happens? The lack of action may be more familiar. For example, few people have enough savings to pay bills and buy food for any length of time without the prospect of a regular income. When people do lose their job they can be surprised to discover they do not have an up to date CV and perhaps lack up to date training that would have maintained relevant skills and put them in a good position in the job market. It is a situation nobody wants to be in.

Practically, there are simple checks to minimize the likelihood of something happening. Taking the two examples above, ask – what is needed to keep it 'safe'? The answers are sometimes easy: a wallet can be kept in a secure pocket or handbag and at work someone can be punctual, productive, and accountable, essentially keeping to task and giving no undue reason to lose their job. In reality both losing a wallet and losing a job are unlikely to be common events and may not occur over the space of several years or even a lifetime, but we still prepare. It is a bit like a vaccine.

We prepare because the impact is something we really do not want to incur.

It is an important step to work to avoid risk, but risk is by nature about something unknown, but with *some* probability, which means sometimes these things do, or could happen. When something does happen, all the effort in the world to prevent risk still does not mitigate its impact. Prevention and mitigation are separate. They may cross over with one another, but not necessarily and they need to be considered separately. Prevention along with taking the steps to mitigate and counter any negative impact is the only way to actually minimize or eliminate the overall risk.

These processes need to be assessed on a case by case basis. With the wallet scenario, it was already something that would only have a minimal impact overall and there are not really additional steps beside those of prevention to take in advance. Where there is the possibility of a large or severe impact, this is when we need to prepare, acting *before,* not just to prevent but also to mitigate the impact of whatever could happen. For example with the scenario of losing a job, someone would need to actively save money, work and develop their professional networks, and make a genuine B-plan for getting another job. Doing these would mitigate the risk and ensure any adverse effects would be considerably lessened should they found themselves without a job tomorrow. Both prevention and mitigation take forethought, planning, time, and effort.

In short, people tend to overestimate things that do not matter and underestimate the things that do. We sometimes let the little things get in our way and do not notice or deal with the things we should. When thinking about our capabilities and what is possible, identifying, understanding, and mitigating risk is important.

Skills as developing capabilities

Ok. I have imagined, dreamed; I have vision and I see possibilities. I have thought about the risks – which means I have mentally visualized the situation, and importantly imagined myself in the situation. Now comes the time to pull up the slouchy socks inside those welly boots (rain slickers) and start walking to build skills.

It is a leap for anyone to go from vision to reality and that is what development is all about. It's like making a print of an old photograph. It used to be that the conditions had to be set up in the dark room, with only a special black light that oddly gave a red glow. (A black glow would not really make sense, would it?) Then it was a carefully calculated process of first exposing the photographic paper to the image and then placing the paper in different trays of chemicals – the developer, the stabilizer, and then hanging it on a line carefully to drip dry – all in the dark of that black light. When I used to do this with my father we had a little timer and I stood on a footstool so I could reach the paper with the plastic tongues. He would explain and very carefully I was allowed to do some of the processes. It was magic as the paper would change in the different trays. Not too much time in one or it would not balance. Not too much time on one aspect of skill development or we overbalance too. It is fun to watch us change, like the paper, as we see the image begin to appear.

It is an immeasurable difference from thinking of something you have not done before to doing it. Before the smell, before the taste, before these happen, I cannot begin to describe what it is to be in the situation. It can be so exciting and unexpected. As I write, woodsmoke from the farm opposite wafts in through my window at home. I can describe what it is like because I am experiencing it, and you could listen and soak the story in, but until you know it too, for yourself, it will always remain a story - a shadow for you. Skills are like that. When we experience them they become real; they grow like new colours in our artistic paint box and then we can use them in familiar and new settings to create and express what we will.

From that first thought of 'ok, I can do this', the skills need to be identified; processes sought; situations to develop them need to be created. It is not like having a list that gets crossed off as each aspect is accomplished. There is a difference between learning skills in isolation and being able to integrate and apply skill. This is more complex than the initial identification of what to learn. It requires us to continually engage with the idea and quest of development, and thus pushes each of us to do more than simply what we can at first imagine.

How can we be responsible for more than we can imagine? In my undergraduate studies I was very fortunate to have a class with the ethnomusicologist and jazz performer Paul Berliner. He had us all read two books about extremes in society: *The forest people* and *The mountain people*. In *The Forest People* there is a story of a man who is taken from the forest for the first time, to a high lookout point and looking at the prairies below the forest he asks, why are there so many insects? He was looking at herds of elephant and antelope, but he had never seen animals at a distance and so could not fathom what he was seeing. When it was explained, he began to understand. We are like that too, but sometimes we do not think to question what we see as being new or other than what we expect.

Noticing capabilities begin to become abilities brings us into a process of real learning, and we need to keep looking and asking, as otherwise we only know how to see so far in front of us. Beside looking farther ahead, we are in the midst of the work, the activity, the change, and that makes it harder to recognize. It is easy to take in the story of the man who lived n the jungle and think aw, what a quaint story, how sweet and innocent of him! But we are exactly the same. Who of us can look at the stars and understand a fraction of the distances between what we connect up as familiar constellations? Those individual stars are lifetimes apart and we cannot begin to fathom any of what or where they really are, not in our familiar terms. That is not to say we cannot see beyond – in fact we can and do everyday, it is just important to know that we do not know everything and we need to actively keep looking and learning in order to grow and develop beyond that old familiar that we already know.

One area where we do look beyond and we adapt to deal with all sorts of predicted and unpredicted happenings is driving. Driving through the countryside does not tend to alarm people. There is no problem with the fact that the scenery changes. First there is a barn and then a row of houses, and then a field followed by a dip in the road and a line of trees. It is all ok and nobody is shouting as each new thing passes. There is no bother of the light changing or the camber of the road being slightly bumpy, and even oncoming traffic does not phase those in the car. We are in a state of expectation and readiness to deal with a certain level of unknown and this allows us to cope and adapt in real time. We essentially are constantly assessing and reassessing in order that we can (literally) move forward in a smooth and controlled manner. Isn't that exactly what we hope to do when developing skills?

Our sights are always set ahead of us, even beyond the horizon to look out for what might be coming next. We have to be like that otherwise, if we just looked immediately in front of the car, we would crash. Progress would be impossible. Looking just in front of where you are means you have a very clear view of that one task right there, but there is no sense of how that fits in the wider context – what came before and what comes after. With eyes just in front of the wheels, moving forward can be overwhelming and we are likely to have to stop every time we want to do any moving in order to reposition ourselves.

It is the same with skill development, when we do tend to look right in front of our noses, we may accomplish that one aspect of the task, but it is unlikely that there will be considerable progress. Sure we need to glance here and there, just like driving, but keeping our eyes on the horizon and a mind that looks for and expects new things will help ensure we progress. Putting the pedal down might mean it's a bumpy road sometimes, so it is always a good idea to buckle up!

Risk (mis)understood: When does it matter?

In the morning when I am standing at the kitchen sink reaching for the sponge to wash up the pan I used to cook breakfast, I am thinking a thousand things and few of those thoughts have to do with the soap, sponge, or the pan. I really do not give any of the process a second thought. Instead I am on autopilot reaching for the soap while looking outside to see the birds hopping about, and I am thinking not about washing but about how the birds are not quite sure if I am a part of the scenery or if I can actually see them through the window.

Is there a risk to washing up? I guess so. I could drop the sponge, splash water on myself, or spill the liquid soap, but these all cause very little in the way of consequences. They have little impact beyond my getting soggy or a bit bubbly. If I spill, I can clean it up. It is only soap and water after all.

Wouldn't it be funny if people actually did not mind about the little things? Can you imagine spilled milk and nobody crying? Colouring outside the lines? This idea of little things that do not matter could be extended across a continuum where the consequences do become increasingly more real. Moving from colouring outside the lines to mowing the lawn crooked to driving outside the lane lines makes a difference and there are obvious risks when cars fail to observe the rules of the road. With most things, and even with driving there is a context where every detail matters and other settings where it just doesn't matter in the same way. Driving the dodge'em bumper cars at an amusement park is a place where nobody follows rules. Well there is no road for a start and the construction of the cars is such that the impact of a bump is absorbed so no injury is caused, just a bump. That is not the normal setting for driving and it is the context for the task that makes all the difference.

Whatever the task, the full context must be considered, and this includes any imposed values or criteria by whomever is involved. Sometimes these do not align with a simple analysis of the task divorced from the particular environment. For example spilling some tea or coffee onto a saucer as you deliver the drink to someone has potentially no consequence in your home, but in the context of being a restaurant server, spilling a customer's drink could cost you your job. Likewise misspeaking and twisting your words can be a silly thing. The Oxford warden, Reverend William Spooner famously mixed up parts of his words when he said things like "The Kinquering Congs Their Titles Take". He was referring to the title of a hymn about conquering kings, and nothing negative but giggles and a list of supposed other silly sayings came from it. In another setting, however, making mistakes with words can be the difference between having a document or a spoken audition or presentation accepted or rejected. Unchecked typos could mean failure, even if the meaning is still conveyed. I recently prefaced a letter by saying that I wasn't going to write a tomb. I meant tome. I meant I was not going to write a lengthy profound letter. What an excellent typo, but oh how I was glad it was in a private communication and not in a book proposal letter. Knowing the requirements and implications of the specific task or event is essential.

When considering risk, it is important to find out what is involved so each case can be individually assessed. Sometimes people know what is involved yet they allow their emotional and personal perspectives to bleed into and overshadow the clarity of understanding the actual impact something could have and then choose to disregard what would be considered a truth. People are afraid to fly but will readily get in a car to travel even though flying is a far safer a mode of transportation. It does not add up. In the language of risk, we are not what are called 'rational actors' when we make these twisted decisions. Sometimes we disregard the risk and other times we are simply ignorant. It serves us well to understand in a level-headed way so we can act. Asking, researching, understanding, and coming to terms with what risk is gives us a better view of what to do. It does not mean irrational worries will go away.

There are plenty of activities in life that do indeed matter, but we do not devote the relevant attention, precaution, or care toward the way we engage with or avoid these activities and this behaviour demonstrates how people regularly misunderstand risk. Take smoking. Thousands of people regularly reach for a cigarette even though smoking accelerates death. It is not even a possible risk, it is a certainty that smoking actually damages the lungs. Now this is a particularly simple and complex example because it is a fact that smoking kills and causes cancer; these things are readily known and printed in big letters on the labels here in the UK. If that weren't enough to make someone wary of the risks, there are other aspects of smoking that people generally do not realize, and if they had this knowledge it would impact decisions to pursue the task. The lungs are peculiar; there are no pain receptors in the lungs, and this means that the body does not present what would otherwise be a normal reaction to the self-imposed damage of smoke inhalation. People cannot feel the pain that would exist if it was a cut, and if the impact was immediately seen and felt, people might genuinely think twice about smoking. That is a slightly graphic example, but it demonstrates the point poignantly and raises the importance of knowledge and understanding.

There is a need to understand the physical risk inherent in situations and the very different but still important risks associated with situations themselves. These could be not completing tasks to a certain level as part of a job. Beyond these there are the things we fritter away our time and energy worrying about and not doing. Things like: 'Oh, I didn't talk to that person because, they might not like me. I could never write to them. I could never present my work in public. I wouldn't dare say that out loud.' It is crazy how the self gets in the way of the *can* even before we get to the *yes*, by pretending there is risk when it is imagined. If we treat even one of these situations rationally and actually asses it for risk and see there is little or no actual impact, then perhaps there's a way to set aside the doubt and be that rational actor.

Outcomes

Throughout learning there are processes to own, direct, guide, and notice and there will be times when the outcome is tangibly demonstrable, as in a thing you make like a house or a cake, but the building of the unseen personal attributes that cannot be directly measured is also very valuable. This section is titled outcomes – *plural*. The starting point to understanding outcomes is there is not one singular finish. There could be, but that would not be the type of outcome that is born out of possibility and capability, but out of directives and does indeed tick a box. The outcomes from the *can* are something you create.

Outcome is a deceptive word, full of implied baggage of goals and measurables. Does perception even have a place when talking of outcomes? If the outcome is about doing what it says on the tin, then this is a road to certainty instead of the concept of possibility.

Ideals

An outcome does not have to be a right or wrong answer, a yes or a no. Knowing how to mix just the right consistency, whether cake icing or the mortar of builder's scree can make all the difference in the overall quality of what you make, and of the outcome. Those skills come with confidence, a bit of yes. How do you know that you have built your yes? It comes with firm answers to the questions *can I?, would I?, have I?* and we see it, even if the physical measurement of yes is not obvious, when the annotation, articulation, and hesitation of steps toward that outcome melt away and we do with a sort of natural grace. Then there is not only an ownership of skill and process, but of the application to the task as well. We start to see self-efficacy in action.

Sometimes the outcome is not a thing at all, but the outcome is that flow-like state of becoming. With music there are stages of learning. As Keith Swanwick says in his book *Teaching music musically,* that we move from the artefact (the sheet music) to the concept (the music itself), from creating tones to tunes. Then when skills are mastered in a musical performance there is a sense neither reading nor performing, but of becoming and allowing. Some people say music flows through them. I say yes, the music can flow through you, but there is more to it as someone becomes more than competent with the skills involved in that creative process. There is a part of the delivery process that involves allowing, where the boundary between you, the instrument, and the music seems to melt. As a performer you become more than process and could not be reduced to any specific action or skill set, but the outcome is an amalgamation quite like alchemy; you as musician, in essence, become the music. For you the outcome is an experience and for the listener the outcome is the creation of something tangibly perceptible as musical communication. Whether you have personally been on the artistic performer end or the audience listener end of this process, chances are you have experienced music and witnessed a performance where the artist just seemed to *be* a part of the music. The existential psychologist Rollo May described this with the artwork of the painter Cézanne:

"The new world which Cézanne reveals is characterized by a transcendence of cause and effect. There is no linear relationship in the sense of 'A' produces 'B' produces 'C'; all aspects of the forms are born in our vision simultaneously – or not at all. ... He painted the *being* of space rather than its *measurements*." - R. May, *Love and Will*, p318-19.

The creativity, the embodiment of capability through possibility, was not about something tangible at all, but about the creation of a concept through a new medium. Now, not everyone is going to have outcomes like *that*, but we should maintain an open enough mind that we *could*. Part of the yes that underpins self-efficacy gives us that resilience to allow for both expectation and deviation. It is natural to have some outcomes held in our minds, like I expect by the end of the month to have read that book or to have finished building that shed or writing that report, but sometimes something causes us to alter course. Not having a predestined answer to exactly what we expect allows for more, for different, and for the new. It allows for greater achievement.

Practicalities

Now, do you walk into a project management board room where someone has just given you tens of thousands to produce outcomes and announce that you plan to defy their expectations and transcend individual processes to realize your yes. No. That is not going to get you a ticket anywhere but out the door. You certainly do need to jump the hoops in a formal setting. Remember the parameters set by people, jobs, and society bind us to a point otherwise there would be anarchy. It is important to keep one foot on the ground and directed and measurable goals will have clear criteria by which you can ensure achievement.

There is not one way, and creative and innovative approaches, even to assigned tasks that you 'have to' do, will ensure you choose and use effective methods to tick the boxes you need to so you can move beyond the measured, required outcomes to pursuing more of what you want, whether that means going beyond expectations within the setting of that job or environment or working on your own personal goals and ambitions. The important aspect is to remember to look up, and keep your eyes ahead, looking beyond, because if you only do what is asked of you there may come a time when someone simply says, 'thanks, that will be all' instead of asking you to turn the page. Ensure you are integral to the task, as a key player in its processes and without whom the outcome could not be achieved in the same way. This is a tactical way of writing yourself into future plans through considered planning and with an informed view of risk, your time, effort, and even if that 'plan' involves tasks right in front of you – it is a plan that keeps you looped in for the long run.

It may be that you are not yet in a position to go beyond the boundaries that are set in front of you. Take that practical view. Start with what is right there before looking beyond the horizon; achieve and then move forward.

Moments of conviction and assurance

Yes is more than a belief, a thought, even more than an intention: Yes is an action. Every action has a beginning, a moment when it first becomes and is no longer an idea. Sometimes those moments creep in unnoticed and other times there is a decided leap off the high dive into whatever you are doing. However it happens, catching a glimpse of those moments and knowing you are the one doing it and later noticing when it is done will evidence your capabilities as abilities and reinforce the foundations of your self-efficacy beliefs.

My wall

This morning I woke up to someone posting one of those motivational phrases, or something that was supposed to be motivational about how 'tomorrow is everything' ...and I thought, hang on, nobody 'gets' tomorrow, all we have is where we are, right now, and that is hard enough to realize. Whatever early thoughts were going through my mind, I decided that was the morning I would get stuck into a slightly crazy project. Just inside the front door is a hallway and it was wallpapered several times over the past three decades. I thought, wouldn't it be nice if it could just be

223

stripped and painted. That became my wall.

The wallpaper striper, with its steam powered nozzle did very little with the four layers, and so I put down the machine and got out a normal kitchen knife. I learned how to shave just under a fraction of the edge of the paper, coaxing it away from the old plaster underneath. Sometimes little scraps with only part of a layer would come off like curls of butter and other times I would find I got it just right and get a foot-long stripe all at once.

I cannot honestly tell you what it was that made me start that job. *Why?* There is not really a logical reason. It is hard to believe that professor-cellist me had a sudden urge to become a completely ill-equipped and inexperienced decorator. I had two sides of 10 feet each to work through. Dang. In other projects, and certainly as a student I have really wanted to do something and plugged away at it and felt like I was making no progress. After a few hours of scraping at the wall with the butter knife I can tell you – that was me right there.

I could no more see the achievement than I could make a career out of decorating. It was exhausting and I did not have a mechanism for knowing whether I was making progress or not. This was unlike any situation I had been in before. I did not know how long it would or should take. I did not have the sort of markers I was used to in the other things I did and without a framework or way to notice how I was going, time - and the task - sometimes stretched out before me like an abyss.

That morning and into the afternoon I almost got lost in the 'wallness' of that project and I could not see what I was doing, why, or how far I had come - and for a fleeting moment it was depressing. The dirt (or wallpaper) really got under my fingernails and it seemed like just a lot of pointless scraping at walls.

I found myself looking down, with a half-shredded wall in front of me and a butter knife in my hand.

It was in that moment when the thought of failure crept in and really cast its shadow over me, but when I looked down and I saw all the rubbish, the peelings I had scraped off the wall, it turned into an moment of enlightenment. I could see the evidence of my progress. Scraping the layers off in little bits was not easy, but I did make progress and I was standing in piles of it. (By the way who in their right mind wallpapers a wall, *plasters over* the wallpaper, puts *more* wallpaper, and then paints over that?!?! – This task was a challenge for me and for the butter knife.) When I saw that gloriously affirming pile of yuck on the floor, I started to think about how important those moments of assurance are. It is vital to know where to look and to be able to recognize them when we see them.

How do we know we are making progress?

Where's the evidence?

What do we use as markers?

It takes patience, detailed attention, and persistence.

Enthusiasm is good, and oh sometimes a kick-start is fantastic, but not necessarily rambunctious effort, but gentle, careful, considered and actioned intention will carry us through. Understanding and noticing the small things helps prepare us to be resilient and to be in a position to act when we have those 'wall' moments.

Congratulations

When people say 'congratulations' it is often accompanied by a sense of celebration, whether hands in the air or champagne corks popping. Likewise, if you type congratulations on your phone or as a social media message, the word comes with animated images of confetti and balloons. Someone must have thought that was an acceptable and expected response to 'congratulations', but what is it for and what does it mean?

Over the months of writing this book, I would sometimes relay my progress on the current section or chapter to a friend, reporting something like '9395 words so far', and once or twice I would see in reply: Congratulations!

It looked so strange to me. I wondered why would someone write that? What have I done? I didn't feel like I had *done* anything. I didn't know how to acknowledge and accept that I had made progress, and certainly did not know how to celebrate it. This has to do with perspective, perception, and understanding. Somehow there was a mismatch between the task, the (assumed) external value of the task, and any personal acknowledgement and value of accomplishing the task. In everyday life we have almost imposed societal values for things. Things cost money, and a price tag is a value of sorts, but I don't love someone £4.50 worth. It would be a mockery to suggest anything like that. The difficulty comes in matching, well not matching, but working around or beyond the external scales that are all around us. There is no absolute with achievement, with what we value, or with what reassures us. A word comforts someone, whereas another person requires the touch of a hand, and someone else looks only to the footprints they leave behind to reassure them of their progress. For each of us the edge of want and need is personal and changes. For me the accomplishment of writing was not in the volume of text, even though that is what I had quantified when describing what I had done. My accomplishment was the public, articulated externalisation of ideas, and that is far more difficult to put into numbers or simple words. Once I found it and named it, I could feel a sense of accomplishment and know I had achieved something.

The key question is *what* – what have you done? – where the 'what' is not necessarily a thing or the obvious answer either. Writing a book is not about the physical item for me in the same way that playing a concert is not about the pages of music, but it is about the lived experience of performance and the possibility of connection it affords both for the player and with the listener. Perhaps it is also like that saying that the cook is pleased when the people eat their food. It is not about the food as some created object simply be admired. When people say congratulations for x, it is not actually about 'x', but about something behind it, to do with it, around it, but oh it is difficult to know and name exactly what it is. The person saying congratulations might not really know exactly what it is, and you might not either, but it is important to find it.

The encouragement of others, through words, gesture, and action is invaluable. Reassurance through concrete results – the cake, the book, the house you built, the road you travelled – is also vitally valuable. Recognising and knowing what you have done, naming it and claiming it for your own allows you to ascribe value to it. This whole process traces capabilities as they move from imagined possibility to realized ability, and as we first recognize and then value our achievement, we reinforce our self-efficacy beliefs. We see the yes.

CHAPTER EIGHT
Moving Forward in the Now

In this chapter practical tasks and questions are set out for you to do so that you can see how you fit in with where you are and can see the possible courses of action in a situation.

The decision and judgement making process is unpicked and analysed with everyday practical examples. Our perception, skills, capabilities, expectations, and risk are weighed and balanced as we understand how our thinking works. First we find and recognize the 'can', and then we move forward to act, transforming the 'can' into a 'do'.

One day I woke up to one of those cliché proverbs on a calendar, the kind where you rip off a paper square each day to reveal a new quote. This one said: "There are two things you can never change – yesterday and tomorrow." It gave me reason to pause.

One of the hardest things in life, for me at least, has been realising I can't change people. What I mean by that is simply no matter what good advice there is to give, alternate course that could be, no matter what the possible benefits – I cannot make someone else *do*. It could be... If only they would change their job, change their diet, stop drinking, do something more, do something less... whatever it is– I'm sure we've all had those *I wish* *if only* thoughts about someone we cared for. Has there been something you have wanted or tried to change in someone else? Did *you* change it or did they? Even if they did what you said, **they** made the change. No matter how much we want it to be true, ultimately the decision to make a change has to come from within.

At that moment it dawned on me. This desperate desire, this urge to correct course is as much about me as it is about someone else. It is far easier to run on a treadmill and look out the window at the other people rather than looking at myself and realize I may not be going anywhere fast. It is so much harder to see where you are and where you could go, and now is the place where it all stops. Suddenly stopping running without awareness certainly means falling off that treadmill, because it's going to keep going and often the gym floor (the place where you fall) is quite hard. Even when you can see where you want to go, it can still be a challenge to be in the now.

When I was at university studying to be a cellist there was nothing I wanted to do more than learn. I was so very hungry to learn and I was aware that the other students had all started far younger than I did, and they were so much farther ahead than I was. There seemed to be so many different nows and I found it very hard to focus on where I was at that moment instead of comparing myself to others. There was a famous piece of research that came out just about then by a team led by someone called Ericsson, about how many hours of practice it took to be a professional. They said it took 10,000 hours and well, I had I guess a few hundred. That really felt like nothing. When I compared myself to others I had no ground to stand on, and one day one of my classmates, who definitely did start when he was 3 years old, and had done his 10,000 hours at least once before entering university, said to me – *'why don't you stop complaining and just practice?'* His point was simple: I could dwell on what I didn't have or I could deal with the now. I chose to deal with it and oh I practiced. I practiced like there was no tomorrow, and it could be said that I went slightly over the top at times.

Seeing where I was and where I wanted to be was part of the picture. The human aspect of now means that processes take time. Even today I am surprised on some days by how much or how little I am able to do in the space of a day. Some days my body tells me, whoa – you need to rest because you know, there's been precious little sleep in your life lately. – and I have to obey. Without a healthy body it is very difficult to let your healthy mind run free. I learned this through another means at university. Being young and clever and ambitious and all the things that you are when you are 19, I thought, *'right! I need to practice, and I have X hours in the day.'* I took stock of what else I needed to do in the day and came up with the two basic things of eating and sleeping. That was it. So perhaps I could maximize my practice time if I was economic with the time spent on other things?

I knew I needed sleep and would practice until I needed sleep – as in fell asleep in the lounge just outside the practice rooms, but eating, I thought maybe that could be condensed. My solution (yes, I really did this) was to be really healthy with my eating (so far good) and I bought 1.5lbs of broccoli from the very healthy Davis Street Market because vegetables are good for you. I thought that if I sat down early in the morning and ate all the broccoli at once, I could get my day's eating out of the way and then I could concentrate on practicing with a really healthy mind. I would save loads of time and that would be great. The only problem was that is not the way that bodies work. If you have ever eaten that quantity of broccoli, you will know that first it gives you a heck of a tummy ache about an hour later and also about three hours later, guess what happens? You are hungry. Really hungry. So yes, I found myself walking over to the student union shop mid-morning to buy my favourite chocolate chip cookie, just like every other day, despite my super-green broccoli-powered plan.

The now takes navigating. If you think you can outsmart now and bend it to your whims, it just ain't gonna happen. We control many things, but not the nature of the moment.

There is an analytical perception of what is around you, and the awareness of what you want. The ways to move forward are not the sort of things any of us can necessarily see clearly.

You can't see it when you're in it.

Just after sunset you can see a clear sky change. It changes from daylight blue to other things, and it is not obvious what colours are about to happen when, and it takes time. There's a word for that – crepuscular. I used it once in the last chapter, because it's a great word, but not a frequently used word. I remember learning it in school, in some vocabulary workbook that had words, their Latin or Greek roots, parts of speech, and examples in sentences. When I came across this oddity, I didn't know what it was so I did what I thought everyone does – I just said it like some similar word in my mind. Crepuscular became chrysalis – the caterpillar cocoon thing. I remembered it because the caterpillar 'changes' and out pops a butterfly. The sky does that too, but with no crunchy slimy birth transformation – just pure colours that imperceptibly shift from ordinary to unbelievable to blossom to glow, somehow giving the light from the no longer visible sun to the emerging stars. The thing is, when you're in it, you hardly notice all that, not at once.

Until there is something to hold on to, some element of perceptible change, the other qualities of now happen – exist and change - both so quickly and so constantly that unless we step outside, we can't see them. That's a chicken and egg situation where the answer is to be a cake – and that abstraction is one step too far for most people to do on an everyday basis. (There is an egg in the cake, but it has been transformed beyond anything it initially was or would become on its own.) We can hold on to some things when we anticipate their arrival. Some time after the sun set, bits of the sky between thin hints of cloud wisp shifted to duck egg blue, and green – the sky turned green. A smoothness came over an area and, like the edge of the finest detail paint brush, a line of the newest crescent moon appeared. Once I saw it, that moon only grew brighter against the salmon sky. That moment of realisation was all it took and then I could look all around the sky, at the horizon that was still shades of orange and gold, and high up where navy began to cover the lighter shades and still, in an instant, I could go straight to the thin line of the moon. The same happened with the next to appear – Venus and then the very faint Mercury, fainter than the prick of a needle in the sky. I could see it.

Knowing where to look, expecting what to see, and being willing to stop and wait as the change happened meant that I could both be there to experience and witness these things. I did have to work to spot them at first, and my eyes would go back and forth, scouring the nothing, but I persisted even though it got darker and colder, and there they were.

An Exercise in knowing your story:

The idea of now and the experience of now can be shown through a simple exercise. What were you doing just before reading this? In those moments, what were the actions? Think about them and write them down - actually write them down on paper and then come back to this for the next step.

Now think about what your intention was while doing them. Were you focused on them or were they things to get out of the way so could get on to doing something else? Write a sentence or two about your intentions while doing them. This time, while writing, I would like you to notice the act of writing. What does it feel like to shape and create the words on the paper, turning them from thoughts into some physical representation of you, what you want, and what you did.

This feeling is a little bit of tasting the now. There was a conscious awareness of what you were doing. It couldn't just happen the first time you wrote because you first have to do the thing and then you can know about it as you repeat, recreate, and expand.

There are other ways to expand further. Now you can read what you wrote aloud and it will sound different. The words take on inflection, ring in your ears. You can go further still and read it to someone else, and then the performative nature of the context adds something, as does the sharing with someone else. With each different iteration you expand your peripheral vision of now.

Getting to the now through YOUR story

With each thing you do, you will have your own story.

Stories are easier than direct observations because they take you into a time of before, where you have been before and are comfortable. Through the (re)telling of your story, you can learn about your now. Just jumping into now is too challenging sometimes, and not everyone can readily snap into being in the now, as well as understanding it, and being able to articulate it all at once. People aren't really taught how to do the introspective reflection of now.

The *cultural* convention is to protect, withhold, and have carefully crafted, separate selves that are not shared. If I were to ask someone, to ask you for example, to tell me a story you might. If you perceive me as a threat, think I am being too invasive then you could easily say- *no, my life is none of your business.*

But when does one person's story become someone else's business? The answer is only when the teller decides it is. People *allow* you to hear their stories. The teller has agency, and whether asked for a story or simply unprompted, *they* make the decision to effectively allow someone else to witness that part of their *self.* The teller may not be aware of what they are letting out or who they are letting in, but they are the ones who decide to tell. The listener then can choose to receive the story or not, but the listener cannot *take* the story.

Why is this important for you and me? The idea of telling a story to yourself allows you to see and experience that introspection. Through familiar stories, people swim in introspection and an outwardly understandable part of the self becomes apparent. However, it is a challenge to make sense of these stories sometimes. Even on their terms, some people perhaps haven't considered themselves from any particular vantage point and have never articulated any notion of 'self' or self-efficacy either to themselves or to anyone else.

Ok, people in everyday life do not often ask us to *'tell them a story'*. I always did as a child, and one day someone asked me to tell a story back. It was a Friday night, and there were benches and logs around a huge campfire in the grounds of Leeland High School, somewhere in Michigan. I don't think I had ever seen such a large bonfire – you couldn't see across the fire to those on the other side, and I had certainly never been to an event where people told stories *on purpose*. People got up and told stories, spooky stories, funny ones, they held everyone's attention with a poem or tale while walking around the crowd of 50 or so. For some reason, at the end after those who had prepared to speak spoke, when the organizer asked if anyone had a story to tell I got up. I told the story of James Thurber's book *The Last Flower*. It was a favourite of mine then, it tells a simple parable of life, with love, abundance (that becomes a greed of accumulation and competition), the destruction of war and the resulting desolation, and hope (that's the last flower) that blossoms into love again. It was the endurance of the flower that stuck with me from that story.

I had never done anything quite like that before. As I told the story I could feel the heat of the fire and the people's eyes on me, and I was aware then that storytelling was different from ordinary speech, whether I was telling my story or someone else's. Storytelling is not a list or a number, but the whole of the words, the delivery, and the person. The physical clues in my eyes, hands, the pitch and pace of my voice, when and how I breathed, how long I made words, and the choice of words all combine to frame, phrase, and articulate the story. And also, they serve to give a window into my now. Every time I tell a story a bit of me seeps out to tells something of my self – not my self-efficacy, but a glimpse at some truth, one of those found glass treasures on the beach.

We can use storytelling to think for and about ourselves. It would be simpler to ask 'what do you think', and that would be the straight way in, but it is harder that way.

The difficulty becomes putting all the pieces together: the cumulative assessment (the thinking about it), articulation (the telling), and inevitable pause it creates (the fact that you are both teller and listener). This pause not only interrupts the flow of both telling and receiving for those not used to this process, but it makes them aware that they are engaging in self-reflection, which can be like seeing your reflection unexpectedly or hearing your voice for the first time can be startling and result in inhibition. Simply put, people hold back.

The magic of a story is that the teller controls what direct content is revealed, but stories allow, without our realising, for 'other' stuff to leak out. Of course the listener needs to be perceptive, otherwise the story could be taken as only a surface level description, communication of necessary information, like Alexa giving directions, or retelling of historical facts. As we all know from school books, *history is not just facts and is always retold from a chosen perspective*. This teaches us a great deal.

People can learn to directly say what they think, but that takes a willingness to take down many barriers that we have spent years putting up and strengthening, and it requires a trust that the listener will respect the story and the elements of personal truth being shown. The now, the thoughts in process, are exactly that – the *person in process*. Seeing that in others can teach us about the formation and understanding of personality, beliefs, and the wider self in them, and seeing it in ourselves teaches us about who we are. Stories are a powerful tool that can let you in when you can't find or bear to look directly into the mirror of your self.

Changing perspectives: The what and you.

What pieces do you have that you're not paying attention to? Turn the tables. What *can* you do to shifting the balance of perspective to focus on the yes?

When we do get to the core question of looking directly at what we think, even then there are identical versions of this question that get at completely different things. It is far more clear in speech than in reading typed words. Hear these:

WHAT do you think? Is different to: What do *YOU* think?

Asking 'what do *you* think?' is an altruistic question, separated from task. It seeks to find out what is the feeling in your gut, the core essence of your beliefs about whatever it is. It is about you whereas asking 'WHAT do you think?' is related to a task and the answer is likely to be more concrete about things like the timing and mechanics of doing whatever it is and how these things fit together practically.

Generally, those untrained in thinking cannot readily distinguish between the two questions. In practical terms this means the emotive self stays intertwined with the task and as a result we have a blurred understanding that impedes progress in learning and progress in self.

WHAT do you think?

The mechanics of a situation are easier to separate out when you take a step back. Think of a board game. Sitting around the table, each player has a certain vantage point, and the way I view the situation will be slightly different from your view – words may appear sideways because I am sitting on the left edge of the board, whereas you can read straight on, but you have to reach around to take one of the cards from the other side of the board, and at times we both have to reach here or there to move a piece. The what of what do you think, has to do with stepping back and taking stock of those mechanics. What are the physical logistical processes involved? And one more step, yet still without judgement or the personal emotional involvement, what are the physical and mental processes involved? This does involve you, but it can be separated out.

In daily life it is in questioning where we fit in that we can find ways of understanding how to get better at the task or how to do it differently. That is when we see differently. An old friend told me a story of learning and noticing and that moment of realisation that there is more than you know now, even for the simple things. She manages a coffee shop and was telling me how great it is to learn new things. She said the other day she learned this clever detail about the daily routine that completely changed how she looked at things: You can lift the mat by the door and clean under it.

Really?!? Somehow after 22 years working at that company, she had never even considered that was a possibility. Surely those mats are stuck down, and why would you ever try to lift one? *But why not?* Turning the tables, and looking lets new thoughts in.

I did a project in 2019 where I learned to play a piece of cello music 'out loud' in an effort to answer this very question. As a musician, there is a lot of practice that goes into performing in a concert, and most of this is done behind closed doors and alone. The process is only seen by the person doing it, and then only seen if they look for and notice it. My learning out loud involved documenting every aspect of my learning and making it externally visible. I was very fortunate to have a small group of people from around the world with me on the journey, as a sort of gentle curious gathering of flies on the wall who shared this window into my daily experience. I shared all this online on a purpose built platform. Sometimes people would comment, and I knew they were there. This made me both accountable and careful to actually explain, as none were cellists or professional musicians. They were a school teacher, a writer, a mother who made crafts with textiles, a student, a poet, and a few more. To this day I have never met any of them in person, but their presence was felt.

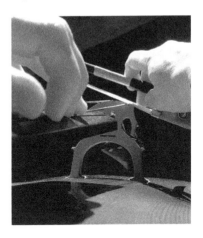

Every day I did what any cello player would; I picked up the cello and worked through a bit more of the piece – playing some passages over and over, learning where to put my fingers, hearing, listening, falling over myself as I couldn't quite coordinate the new music between my bow and fingers, and throughout it all I kept time to pause and document each step of the way. I recorded audio, made short video clips of the challenges and new skills, and wrote notes about what, why, and how I spent my time each day. In all my years of learning I had never done this. Yes, I had written things down, but not so consistently, and the result was that I learned more than I had ever done before.

It was like I had been sitting on the side of the board game before, and somehow I got the idea to turn the table and look at it as someone else might do. When I noticed what was happening and spelled it out, there was so much more clarity. That different perspective gave new insights even though I didn't change anything really. There was no sudden regime, no requirement to spend x amount of time doing this or that. I simply did what I did and looked, listened, and payed attention to the physical mechanics of what was happening – in a very conscious way. It was daunting, exciting, and very revealing.

Not everyone will have a willing audience for a task, and I don't suppose I will have that again. It was a unique situation. What it taught me was to pay attention and the benefits that can have.

An exercise in noticing WHAT you think:

You can hold yourself accountable for a task in a similar way. Take an easy thing that you do all the time like washing your hands or putting on your shoes and pay attention. How can you document it? Making a film from start to finish is not ideal, because that is too much at once. Think through the component movements, where you need to go, what you need to get or have, how long it takes and select one of those aspects to show. Select something to explain. Select yet another thing to analyse. You don't need to do this for the whole of the task, but only for parts. For each part that you choose, examine some aspect of it carefully. For example, how do you stand when you do this? Are you hunched? Do you lean on something? Notice and think through this aspect of the task. Then actively make a note of it, either write something down or record yourself speaking about it.

That was step one. Now do it again the next time you happen to engage in that activity, but this time slightly differently. If the task was putting on your shoes, this time notice which hand reaches for the shoe first. If there are laces which one goes on top? Can you pause these automatic processes enough to be with them as you do them? Feel that, and note it down. That is the *what* you think.

What do YOU think?

In my cello project the documentation continued day after day and culminated with a public performance on day 128. In those days there were lots of ups and downs, physically taxing moments, exhausting sessions, frustrating times where I intellectually understood what I should do because I had analysed the **what** already, but aspects of what *I* thought got in the way. This was documented as well, by writing about the human aspect of the process with my opinion and how I felt: what I hoped for, what pleased me, and when I was genuinely struggling. I wrote down when I didn't want to practice, and even what I did instead, which was sometimes to spend hours doing something completely unrelated like picking raspberries. Learning this particular piece of music was my Everest and it had obvious challenges, perhaps more so than routine everyday tasks, but that does not mean that thinking about everyday activity is any less valid or useful to learning and understanding the processes of our self.

Thinking about the *I* in your thinking, your personal attitudes, opinions, and emotions, is more complicated than noticing whether you tie a shoe with the left lace first or use your left hand to turn on a tap. We are intertwined with these thoughts and it would be silly to suggest separating yourself from them – noticing and owning them on the other hand is something you can do.

An exercise in what YOU think:

In a very similar way to the previous exercise where you noted the details of what you were doing, this time when doing the task take the time to notice how you are. How do you feel about it, before you begin? While you are in the middle of the task are you fatigued, bored, pleased? Do you notice progress or are you consumed with the details? Are you *in* the task or are you so familiar with it that it can be done on autopilot and you can really notice?

It is more difficult to do this sort of noticing because you are in the midst of it, and it does mean taking a mini-pause to notice. In order not to disrupt the actual task, you have to simply notice, not judge, take a note, and carry on. This may feel strange, but taking more of a pause is likely to break the natural flow of what you are doing.

You can do this again – perhaps not every time you do the task, but if you remind yourself first with either noticing before or after how you feel, then you will learn to notice in a way that becomes less and less disruptive, and then you can move those questions into the task itself.

As you get good at asking both **what** you think and what *you* think with simple tasks, you can integrate these questions and the associated noticing into more challenging or specialized tasks. Looking at what you notice is your turning the tables. You read the cards from a different angle, and even if you make the same moves your understanding and awareness will be wider and more informed, leaving you more secure in your self.

Letting in the now

The map.

Any judgement, an assessment of a situation or task, thought or spoken word, takes time, space, and attention from us to sort out. I will use the word assessment instead of judgement, simply because judging very often has the associative baggage of wrongfulness. In the judicial system people are said to be innocent until *proven guilty*. Culturally we seldom cast judgement to celebrate, however we assess to learn and grow. How we frame things for ourselves matters.

This holds true when thinking about our lives, the how, when, where, with whom, and what we do. In the morning over a cup of coffee you may well say to the person sitting opposite you, *'How does your day look?'* or *'What do you have going on?'* and most likely they will know exactly how to answer. The calendar on my phone has several different colours for events – personal, family, work – and I can see my day in front of me. It is all mapped out right there, and the default is to vault from one scheduled item to the next and think we know where we're going. Sometimes we assume a map or schedule actually does much more than it says on the tin. There is certain information presented in a map, but a map does not tell us where to go or even where we are going. It shows us what is there and the recorded information. The 'what is there' on a map or calendar is an artefact, a collection of constructions – past, present, and planned for the future. We can see roads, buildings, and natural landmarks in our lives. We will have built up to achievements, and yes, met with natural events that were our personal mountains or valleys. Unlike our experience, a calendar or map can also show places we have not yet been. The calendar has blank dates. We know exactly how many days it is until October or the next birthday or until you go to see your friend, but the information that is missing in the map or calendar is the process.

We can read the calendar with a sense of expectedness and security of already knowing what there is to do. Somehow it is like we assume there is more information than just the what and possibly the when and where. We are different to a map, and when we do make this comparison, we sometimes do not realize the weight inherent in the lines of our personal map. If I read the map of my face in the mirror I see various lines, one from a smile, one from worry, and another that is no less deep but far less sinister from the pillow after waking up first thing in the morning. The sleepy line from the pillow will fade but the others don't necessarily, and as we move forward it is important to acknowledge the roads we have travelled to get where we are. I believe in myself because I know I can. I know, in part, because these lines on the map of my face, tell me I so. I can look into my past and see what I have done. Likewise I can reflect internally to see how my self-efficacy has been shaped by the 'roads' to and from my achievements.

You may be blessed with a lovely smooth face, but our hands all have lines on them. Apparently, to those who do read these lines on palms, one hand is the past and one is the future. I wonder where is the now? I do not know about palmistry but would like to use hands as an image. When we approach complex tasks we tend to use our whole selves, physically, and the image can carry forward to the hands as being the past and future: we integrate past skills and future hopes to build the now. Imagine two hands working with clay on a potter's wheel. Skill is needed as well as guidance and vision. If our working is too heavily laden with a focus on skills and the way they were learned or executed in the past, that 'past' hand could have too strong a hold and crush the clay. Likewise, if in working that clay we were only vaulting so strongly toward the goal without the balance of skill the clay would never take shape.

Letting in the now has to do with acknowledging, and sometimes dealing with the past experiences of 'then'. These are how you got to where you are now. There will be roads taken, skills built through successes and failures along the way, and it is a task in itself to allow these cornerstone events that helped build us to remain in the past instead of holding on to them. We do bring the skills and confidence gained from them into the present. Then we can each assess where we are now and have that realistic view of how to proceed. Keeping our goals in mind is important, as without the direction from goals there would be no future roads to draw or follow on the map.

When you get good at balancing assessment with progress in the now it is like walking, whereby moving one foot at a time we have the freedom of guiding and controlling new directions. We choose the stride and pace while remaining grounded instead of feeling pushed, pulled, or like we are leaping off into the future. Now is not always about walking and yes, you can certainly jump forward and you may well develop the skill to add acrobatics to your routine, but without guidance and skill, attempting these things unaided or unprepared could be pretty risky.

Simplicity

Simplicity is attractive and approachable. Simple words can help us encapsulate complex concepts with accessible images and bypass the cognitive mechanics of understanding that could otherwise baffle us. Eventually we can approach the doing that would otherwise not be obvious or intuitive. For example walking is an easy concept to think of, whether walking the dog, walking to the car, walking to take a book off the shelf, yet to do this we orchestrate hundreds of intricate carefully timed movements to negotiate balance and measure distance in order to move forward just the right way in time and space. Looking in detail it is very complex and there is no way we can or should know all the steps.

When first approaching a task it can be essential not to be overwhelmed with the detail and so we can use metaphor to link what is already known and allow access to understanding. However if you want to become an expert, the simplicity of an overview and knowing only through shadows is definitely second best.

I can explain through music. People see singing as opening your mouth and sound, the voice, comes out. This is of course more complex. It is easier to explain and 'see' with a physical instrument. When I play the cello I sit and the instrument rests on me. There is a mixture of ease and intricate detail. When I say it rests on me, I do not even need to hold it. Each of my hands though, does something different. In the end, you see me 'playing the cello' but there is independence of and synchronicity between my hands down to the most minute level of nuance. They move together, separately, and differently at the same time. One hand's motion precedes the other in order to allow for the aural illusion of smoothness and continuity of sound instead of hearing the separate steps.

The right hand holds the bow, which is the cello's breath. The bow is a finite length and practically every time the direction of the stick of the bow changes as it pulls back and forth over the strings is like drawing new breath. In those moment of changes, the left hand moves, so the fingers are placed on the notes in anticipation, before the hair of the bow initiates the string and releases the sound.

It is simple, yet so complex, and the end result is for someone to hear sound as music, not process or technique. They really never should particularly know the details that go into creating the sounds.

When carrying out a task that we have mastered we let go of the awareness of these complex details. Take reading for example. It is unlikely that you actively *feel* the motion of the eye or the balance of the hands as they hold the text for us to perceive, knowing exactly how far away the text should be, or that we consciously digest the phonetic and structural purpose of the letters and words as they cross our gaze. It is only when something unexpected or beyond our skill set suddenly appears that we slow down, out of necessity to avoid stumbling, and become aware of the process. We can however choose to mine into the detail of any process and focus our attention to assess and improve.

When creating the sound on a cello the bow moves across the string and, conceptually, the goal is to create a tone that is similar to spinning silk, with a thread of sound that is strong yet delicate and has the capacity to become something substantial like a rope or almost imperceptibly subtle like a single thread that we hardly know is there until it brushes past us. The sound produced by the bow is a product of three main technical factors that can be manipulated to create a specific, desired outcome. I can play with varying weight - pressing into the string, or with speed – like the wind, or with a different placement – impacting, in the simplest of terms, the orienting perspective of the sound. If any one of these changes, the nature of the sound changes. These make sense in any setting: Add the speed of an icy wind and even the experience of a beautiful field becomes harsh; Stand on top of a lighthouse and the view of the sea is very different than when swimming in its waves; Press on someone's throat and they can't breathe. Each change has a completely different impact, that will then be heard in the light of people's experience and understanding.

Interestingly, although the bow (in the right hand) is the thing making the sound, the left hand, which is imperceptible in itself, does everything that the western listener initially decodes as the music. The left hand is responsible for the pitch which is the basis for the melodic and harmonic content. When put together it is a bit like saying the cello is a book with blank pages, left hand provides the ink for the words, and the bow sets the type. The origin of the music's grammatical syntax is a combination of the three, comprising timbre, pitch, tone, and articulation.

Indulge me with one further musical example. In sound, contemporary string players tend to use vibrato. This is partly because the ear quickly tires of a sinusoidal tone (did you just slow down there? Wondering if sinusoidal (of sine waves) is outside your normal sound vocabulary and whether as a result you became aware of the process of reading and slowed down to question that word or simply skipped over it?) after a fraction of a second. The gentle oscillation of vibrato keeps the listener interested and gives the impression of motion in the sound. The actual vibrato we hear results form a balance of action between the left and right hands. If the left hand does the wobbling to change the pitch very slightly and the bow catches the sound, by having just the right placement, speed, and weight. If the factors to do with the bow are not optimally balanced, the activity of the left hand will be lost and the listener will not hear the vibrato clearly.

Admittedly, that is quite a technical detail of cello playing, and a casual listener does not *need* to understand or be aware of any of that, but this concept of the depth of understanding relates to most things that we do. The initial understanding of something can seem easy when we just do the thing, and then in learning we do unpick it, but still once that thing is learned, instead of letting it go, we can work so very hard to analyse every morsel of action and process and get in the way. Can you imagine if a chef stopped to overanalyse the fast knifework they do when chopping vegetables? Sometimes experiencing this analysis can be useful, as a learning tool.

Find your balance:

It's your turn. As a practical exercise, consider those three qualities from cello bowing and apply them to a situation in your life.

- **Placement** This is your perspective.
- **Speed** is your pace.
- **Weight** Consider this either the pressure you feel or the presence you bring to the situation.

Take the very ordinary situation of getting a coffee and one by one let's manipulate these ingredients to see what the change in process and outcome is like. Whether you actually get a coffee, juice, or water is up to you, and it is also up to you whether this drink it from your home or from a café or shop.

Placement: How does your experience change if you consider it from the perspective of someone else in the room? This can either be the person serving you or someone else in your house. Paying attention to how they would see the situation, and how they would see you may give you a heightened awareness of your movements, position, interactions, and perhaps even cause you to question how and what you do.

Speed: This will sound like a game and it will either intrigue or stress you. What if you put a time limit on the situation? Either move more quickly on purpose or do the opposite and linger. You could use a musical technique Chopin liked called 'leaping and lingering' where he would basically mix it up and both hurry and then enjoy stasis, musically speaking. Glancing over and dwelling on different aspects of the task will foreground these in your mind's eye. Experience how this impacts your perception and awareness of now.

Weight: You can literally weigh in by entering the space boldly, loudly, and with gravitas. This may be far outside your character, in which you can waft in, being almost invisible. Whatever you are used to doing, explore something different. It does not have to be a polar opposite, but a change will begin to show you the range of expressive experience available to you.

Manipulating any one of these will produce a change. The skilled artist will balance the three as if marbles being rolled on a very large tilting table to avoid holes and gently follow their chosen path. Practice on other situations to see what you can do and how it feels. First we apprehend simple details of what and how, and after decoding it, we all need to work to find the balance between the energy and concentration needed to carry out the skills, to allocate that and then to get to a place where we can let it happen, regaining the initial simplicity. Reading, walking, knitting, driving, - you will have tasks that you do and do well in a state of ease. You may think these are easy. That's the same thought you will have when watching an expert. When you have achieved mastery, it does look and feel easy.

The formula for change

Self-efficacy + Skills + Agency = Change

Self-efficacy, your belief in your capabilities, is your yes. By nature, 'yes' is both a statement and an answer to a question. It does not apply to everything automatically, nor is simply saying 'yes' sufficient. Flinging your arms in the air emphatically and declaring YES! may be an outward show, but means precious little. *Yes what*, exactly? Yes the lights are on? Did you leave the door open? Like the light in the fridge? Well that is not a very good yes?! The kind of yes that goes with self-efficacy is deliberate and focused.

There really needs to be an awareness of what that yes is referring to. The question of *'yes what?'* can be framed in terms of specific criteria and a context. I can jump... *'over that puddle'* is different to I can jump *'from the high dive'*. Understanding the specifics will not only help to answer the question of 'what' but will give you the clarity to articulate your belief. This defining the task means an awareness of what it is and what is required of you. Without that knowledge the yes is unqualified, and little more than a giddy moment. This is level-headed assurance, with a purpose, and promise to your self.

The second part of self-efficacy has to do with

understanding and believing you can also do what is required of you in terms of skill delivery. First is to believe you can do the task – focusing externally on the criterial, situated task, and then is to believe *you* can do all the component skills of the task. To do this we need to ask ourselves: What are the skills? Answering this means both being aware of what the skills are (naming them) and whether or not you personally have these skills. It is possible that you need to gain the skills, and Chapter 5 outlined the processes for learning and checking skill development through the metacognitive steps of self-regulation. When you adhere to learning and are accountable to yourself, which is even more important than being externally accountable for your learning, then *you* can test both mentally and physically to have a secure reality check of whether or not you can do what is required for the task at hand.

Practically, learning and then the assessment of whether you have mastered the component skills of any task may take time and not be as simple as answering yes to the question of 'can you?' Having a realistic view needs to be founded on evidence that you indeed have what it takes for all the requisite parts of the task before you can move on with confidence.

I like to bake and when I came to the UK back in… well half a lifetime ago, I met a really lovely pudding (desert) called profiteroles and years later I decided to learn how to make them. I now have a recipe that I use that I find quite easy, but it had many, many failures before I achieved that ease as I adapted the recipe from several online and in print versions and it finally became my own. Here it is:

- 1/2 cup butter
- 1cup water
- 3 eggs
- 1 cup flour

Those are all the ingredients for the pastry. The recipe has a few instructions, but not many:

Melt the butter. Add the water. Boil. Turn off the heat and add the flour all at once. Mix. Let sit for a few minutes to cool slightly. Add the eggs. Mix. Drop onto a baking tray. Bake in a medium hot oven until golden and risen and then decorate as you like. That really is it.

I leave them whole and drizzle chocolate on top, and if people want to add whipped cream or ice cream they can do that to their own taste.

It sounds *so very simple* but believe me it is easy to fail really hard on this one. There are many recipes that are fool proof, like if you make a basic cake and chuck all the ingredients together, much like a packet mix, it will turn out like a cake. If you mix all these together it will turn out like liquid plaster and never change from a sludge texture no matter what you do. Then if you bake that sludge you get little hard discs that never rise and both taste and look like sink stoppers.

What 'skills' could there be?? Sometimes seeing the skills in a task is easy, but other times there is just a lot to know that is not seen. I'm reminded of being a passenger on a sailboat and watching the water ripple past and having no clue how the winds and currents and tide work with the sails, and just how far the little boat can tilt. Sometimes skills cannot be so easily demonstrated as writing an answer on paper. With this cooking it is all about the way you mix. The butter and water do boil, and then when the flour goes in all at once, the liquid must be still nearly boiling. If it is cool, that's how you get sludge. When the liquid is piping hot, and you mix like fury with a wooden spoon, the flour comes away from the sides instantly and blobs into a neat soft ball in the middle of the pot. The next bit is equally mysterious. The pot has to cool so the eggs do not actually cook when cracked onto the buttery flour dough ball. Eggs splop around like a moat and then the mixing continues in earnest. This mixing counts as aerobic exercise, and the instructions certainly do not imply that.

At first the dough fragments like some floating horrors and it looks like a failure, but this is exactly correct. After yet more mixing, suddenly as if by magic it becomes smooth and has that sought after 'dropping' texture. Perfect. Scoops of this smooth mixture sit on the baking tray, keeping their shape like dollops of frozen sorbet before they at least double in size in the oven. If you do not know about the temperature and the processes the ingredients go through in the mixing, anyone would be forgiven for deciding something went wrong at an early stage. If, however, any flour is added to the mix after that boiling liquid stage it becomes instant sludge.

I know I have the skills because I have approached them, tested them, applied them, and seen the results. That gives me my reality check that indeed I can. Now there are things that I know I can do (in my mind), and I know that physically I can carry out the skills, but would I actually do them? That last step is agency, the conviction, the choice to do it. A big step in being able to do something for real can involve externalising the previous two components. When you know what you can do then you can choose action. Perhaps you feel the need to improve or learn more first, but having taken the time to analyse, you will be able to identify what you need to improve and direct yourself in how to learn more. That too is a choice toward action.

We have looked at abstract and specific examples and by now you can really begin to put these pieces together for yourself in your own situations. The structural formula has these key components and once you grasp these, you can enact change. There is no faking it or bypassing them. It does not work to lie about your self-efficacy; it is part of you, what you think and what you are. You can look into yourself you can either find it already there, or see that you want it and grow the belief and skills. Then you have the tools at your disposal to create genuine possibility.

Making it happen

Now is when you decide what it is you would like to do. What drives you? Where would you like to be? At the heart of it all, when you look at yourself in the mirror, when you look into your mind what do you really think? Do you believe in you? When you find that *yes* what follows is meaning, and a vibrancy in your now, because there is commitment for you, commitment to you, and a commitment to what you want to do. It is all underpinned by self-efficacy. When you genuinely believe *yes I can*, then really somehow you will make it happen.

Remember that you cannot know exactly what is before you, how others will react, and in truth we live in a complex world where there are countless personal, societal, and environmental influences that all contribute to how the events in our lives play out. Even if you know about words, people, and events, their impacts and influences will be real. We are each human, and do not have the predictable solidity of a chair, with an inbuilt tensile strength and a calculated sturdy construction. We experience; we feel; and when we fall there will most likely be tears and a bit of pain. That's what happens when your eyes suddenly see the ground instead of being focused inward on your capability and outward toward the vision of possibility. The thing about really having self-efficacy is that you will get back up and keep walking forward, because even if distracted, you don't forget that goal and the genuine belief that you can. And when you do achieve, through your own agency, you will rejoice and so will those around you. You will be the influence and the impact on yourself and your world around you. In truth, yes I can and yes you can.

End Notes

1. See Downes, S. (2017). *Toward Personal Learning*. National Research Council, Canada. p.287 available online at https://www.downes.ca/files/books/Toward%20Personal%20Learning%20v09.pdf

2. Yes, I do include *all* here, as even the most highly trained professional can improve and widen sights and experiences. There is no real or implied ceiling to perception. Even the limits of physicality are so complex that the interactive nuance of real time situations means that there will be no finite achievement of perception.

3. To read the full article in detail and see the example images from the study, see Cohen, M., & Rubenstein, J. (2019). How much color do we see in the blink of an eye?.
    Available online at: https://psyarxiv.com/enywt/ and for further reading, see Haun, A. M., Tononi, G., Koch, C., & Tsuchiya, N. (2017). Are we underestimating the richness of visual experience?. *Neuroscience of Consciousness*, *2017*(1), niw023.
    Available online at: https://academic.oup.com/nc/article/2017/1/niw023/2970153

4. Yantis, S. (Ed.). (2001). *Visual perception: Essential readings.* Psychology Press.

5. https://www.desertedislanddevops.com/about/ https://www.vice.com/en_ca/article/z3bjga/this-tech-conference-is-being-held-on-an-animal-crossing-island

Further Reading

Within this book several research studies have been mentioned. What follows is a brief description of each of these studies as well as a few other suggestions for further reading on the subject.

William James was a psychologist and philosopher who wrote prolifically and comprehensively. His book *Principles of Psychology* (1890) covers all aspects of life and is often presented in a diary-like way. This is ironic in that he was the one to coin the term 'stream of consciousness', which is one of the themes of his book, alongside emotion, habit, and will. The book is widely available to read for free on the internet.

Here is a copy available from the Archive.org library: https://archive.org/details/theprinciplesofp01jameuoft

Tolman (1948) was famous for his experiments with rats in mazes. He studied external processes and expanded the understanding that behaviour of learning was not merely a predetermined reflex-type response, but a goal-directed activity influenced by several external stimuli. Tolman theorised that animals created mental maps of their surroundings.

Tolman, E. C. (1948). Cognitive maps in rats and men. *Psychological Review, 55*, 189-208.

Albert Bandura introduced the concept of self-efficacy (1977) and defined it as "the conviction that one can successfully execute the behaviour required to produce the outcome" (p.193). This shifted social cognitive theory to focus on the role of an individual's beliefs in determining actions and outcomes. Self-efficacy was first studied in the context of therapy for phobia, and since then researchers have studied these self-beliefs in all areas of life, from education to hobbies to professional contexts.

Bandura, A. (1977). Self-efficacy: Toward a unifying theory of behavioral change. *Psychological Review, 84*(2), 191–215. https://doi.org/10.1037/0033-295x.84.2.191

In his pivotal book *Social Foundations in Thought and Action* (1986), Bandura made it clear that people control their thoughts, emotions, and actions, and importantly, that thought mediates knowledge and action. He set out a reciprocal relationship that is the fabric of human functioning, involving personal, behavorial, and environmental factors.

Bandura, A. (1986). Social foundations of thought and action. Englewood Cliffs: NJ

Ericsson and his colleagues published a paper in 1993 that famously stated 10,000 hours of *deliberate* practice are needed to achieve an expert status. Interestingly, they found an amateur required about 4,000 hours of deliberate practice. This distinction between deliberate and not deliberate is at least as important as the quantity of practice.

Ericsson, K. A., Krampe, R. T., & Tesch-Römer, C. (1993). The role of deliberate practice in the acquisition of expert performance. *Psychological review*, *100*(3), 363.

Tim Urdan and Frank Pajares (2006) edited a book that discusses self-efficacy as a psychological construct, specifically including agency, and go on to advise researchers on questionnaire development protocols for research studies. The book includes advice and examples from prominent researchers, including Bandura himself, and topics span from adolescence through developing toward adulthood.

Pajares, F., & Urdan, T. (Eds.) (2006). Self-efficacy beliefs of adolescents. Information Age Publishing, Greenwich, CT.

Bembenutty, Kitstantas, and Cleary (2013) compiled a very useful book that pays tribute to Barry Zimmerman, who was seminal in introducing, studying, and demonstrating the nature and use of self-regulation. Within this volume aspects of metacognition are explained in terms of self-regulation theory and demonstrated through practical application. The book includes a range of examples and case studies from diverse areas, ranging from various academic disciplines to using aspects of self-regulation to manage chronic disease.

Bembenutty, H., Kitsantas, A., & Cleary, T. J. (Eds.). (2013). *Applications of self-regulated learning across diverse disciplines: A tribute to Barry J. Zimmerman*. Information Age Publishing, Greenwich, CT.

This list is by no means comprehensive, but does give more detail on a few of the specific texts mentioned in this book.

Image Credits

Images in the Introduction (poppy) and in Chapter Four (barbed wire, rainbow, and field and road sign) are by Alan Levine and licensed CC0.

Artwork in the dedication and in Chapter Two are by Catherine Ritchie https://www.catherineritchie.org/

The images in Chapter Two and Chapter Six are historic.

All other images, including the cover, were taken by Laura Ritchie.

In the audio book, all music was composed, performed, and recorded by Laura Ritchie.

Laura does embody this Yes I Can. She very much enjoys speaking, travelling, connecting with people, and helping people connect with themselves and see their possibilities in a new light. She would be very pleased to hear from you. The door is open.

CPSIA information can be obtained
at www.ICGtesting.com
Printed in the USA
BVHW092201190421
605300BV00014B/1606

9 781999 794347